The Hidden Gospel

Once A Mystery But Now Revealed

SECOND EDITION

Dr. David Alan Greene

GraceWord Publishing, LLC
www.gracewordpublishing.com
U.S.A.

GRACEWORD PUBLISHING

Content

Acknowledgements   xi

  1 How We Begin   1

  2 The Fear Of Being Wrong   9

  3 How Firm A Foundation   15

  4 Upon This Foundation   23

  5 Fences   31

  6 The Seed   41

  7 A Peculiar People   49

  8 An Interruption   61

  9 Twelve To One   69

10 No Longer A Mystery   79

11 A Heavenly Inheritance   89

12 An Earthly Inheritance   97

13 Side By Side   107

14 Final Words   121

Resources   131

Other GraceWord Publications   133

About The Author   135

To John & Linda

For the grace of God that bringeth salvation
hath appeared to all men,

- The Bible

Acknowledgements

I would like to express my appreciation to Jon and Susan McMahon for their continual encouragement. Thank you Steve Tackett for always being willing to discuss the biblical text with me. A special thank you to Frances Greene, Melissa Lindsey, Dorothy Locker, and Barbara Pennington who assisted in the preparation of this book.

1

How We Begin

This book is out of my comfort zone, but I think that is a good thing. We should all try something new or learn something out of our comfort zone. I specialize in teaching graduate level students and writing academic books that teach the Bible. This one is not, I repeat not, written for the academic. I intend to walk a person through the Bible and explain it to them in a way that they may not have heard before. When I teach, I want to present the information in a way that is understandable. Whether they accept and believe it is up to them . . . and the Holy Spirit. We all have free will. Each of us chooses to accept or reject what we believe.

As an insurance agent for thirty-five years, I explained policies and coverages to people for a living. It might surprise you that most people have no idea what their policy says. They just trust their agent. I met a few clients who read their policy and called to ask me questions. To them, I tip my hat. Like policyholders who trust their agent to make their insurance decisions for them, most church-goers trust their clergy to tell them what to believe. I would like you to think about this. If I could show you a simple system to read, understand, and enjoy your Bible, would you be interested? You would no longer be dependent upon others to tell you what it says. You could read it and understand it for yourself.

Since Sunday School, I have always loved the Bible. Later in life, I wanted to understand it the same way I could understand insurance policies. I wanted to be able to read it, understand it, and explain it to others. Insurance companies write policies that are approved by the state. They govern the relationship between the insurance company and the policyholder. The Bible was written by God. He inspired men to write down His Word. Its content explains and governs things from God's perspective. God would have written it so that people could understand it, right? Therefore, understanding what the Bible says and what it means is very important. Like policyholders, most believers won't take the time to read it for themselves.

I completed my degrees late in life which allowed me to apply life experience to gain a practical understanding. My approach to anything has always been to first see its structure or framework. In the Bible, we find various agreements and promises God made. These include contracts or covenants, promises, warnings, and prophecies about the future. Like a policy which is a legal document, it can't be changed unless both parties agree. However, with God, He won't ever change anything He said or wrote. That is to our advantage! Once we understand the Bible, we can be sure that it will never change! That certainly makes it worth our time to understand it.

God said He will not change His Word. He warned anyone who does change it. You can read the warning yourself in Revelation 22:18-19. Many are led by others to believe what the Bible says without checking it for themselves. Picture this. Someone bought an insurance policy and later had a claim. The company denies the claim. These people go to the insurance company and say, "Well, my agent said I was covered!" Another might say, "My neighbors said I was covered!" The first thing the company will do is point to the policy and say, "No, look here. The policy says you're not covered." Here is my point. Regardless of who tells you that the Bible says this or that, it is always your responsibility to verify it yourself! This applies to me as well. Therefore, I include Bible text and citations for you. Think of these as the sources where you can fact check the information in your Bible yourself.

There are a lot of wolves in sheep's clothing out there. There is lots of money to be made in man's religion. For that reason, in this book I am going to show you a failproof system to read the Bible and understand it. This is my promise to you. Once you finish this book, you should be able to see the overall framework of the Bible. By using this framework you can understand it and you will enjoy reading it more and more. It is my goal for you to ask and answer this question: "What does the Bible say?"

If you're like most people, you'll look around to see what everyone else is doing. Don't do that! They may say the Bible says this or that. However, it can't be true unless it agrees with the whole Bible. Many evangelical churches appear to preach from the Bible. Be careful. They read several verses from the Bible. Then, they use it as a springboard to talk about anything and everything else. This is the reason most people don't understand the Bible. They present snapshot photos and not the whole picture. What if we start by understanding what God says in His Word by seeing the whole picture? Once you do, you will be surprised just how many preachers and teachers don't see the whole picture. However, you will.

I believe there are two obstacles that prevent people from understanding God's Word. First is organized religion. Organized religion is created by man. It is designed to perpetuate itself and creates for its followers a dependency. Their goals are (1) to increase attendance and increase their income. Putting that aside, the second biggest problem is this. In this present age, salvation by God is way too simple! If the people find out how simple it is, then it is immediately dismissed as "foolishness!"

The Bible does speak about "foolishness" which is not what you may think. It is the most educated people who think the simple message of the Bible is, well, "foolishness." Let's take a look at some verses where God uses this word. 1 Corinthians 1:18-25:

> 18 **For the preaching of the cross is to them that perish <u>foolishness</u>; but unto us which are saved it is the power of God.** 19 **For it is written, I will destroy the wisdom of the wise, and will bring to nothing the understanding of the prudent.**

20 Where is the wise? where is the scribe? where is the disputer of this world? hath not God made foolish the wisdom of this world? 21 For after that in the wisdom of God the world by wisdom knew not God, it pleased God by the foolishness of preaching to save them that believe. 22 For the Jews require a sign, and the Greeks seek after wisdom:

23 But we preach Christ crucified, unto the Jews a stumblingblock, and unto the Greeks foolishness; 24 But unto them which are called, both Jews and Greeks, Christ the power of God, and the wisdom of God.

25 Because the foolishness of God is wiser than men; and the weakness of God is stronger than men.

What you will learn in this book may be considered "foolishness" by others. However, as we read in verse 25 above, "the foolishness of God is wiser than men."

Most Christians believe all the Bible was written "to" them. Now, wait a minute. You might reply. "Of course, I know the Bible was written to Christians!" Wait a minute. Look at the small words in italics. The Bible was written "for" everyone. This is true. However, that doesn't mean that the Bible was written "to" everyone. Did you catch the difference? I know this may seem petty. However, it is a bold statement at the state. I needed to get your attention. We have to separate from the pack and start thinking on our own with the help of the Holy Spirit.

To get the most out of this book you will need to do something as you sit reading it. You need to put aside what you think you know about the Bible. This includes all the stuff – the bits and pieces – you've collected over the years from different people. We are going to start by introducing a system or framework. Like building a sturdy bookcase, this will allow you to go through the clutter and decide what you will keep. As you organize your beliefs you can test them to see if they are of value or not. We all have stuff we don't know what to do with. So, we keep it and put it with all the other clutter. You may have a throw-away pile when you're done. Take comfort in this. You alone are the one who decides which beliefs you will keep and which ones you won't.

2

The Fear Of Being Wrong

Do you remember the stories of the Pharisees in the gospels? Many Christians see the Pharisees as evil. They were the religious men who were highly educated. They had the equivalent of a doctorate in Mosaic Law. For centuries, they were taught by brilliant men who had been taught by brilliant men who had been taught by brilliant men. Somewhere along the line, they lost the plot. Yet, Scripture remained unchanged. Then, along comes Someone Who tells them that what they are teaching is wrong. That did not go over well. Jesus was challenging the established religion. This Person was the Son of God. He was, and is, and will always be the Word of God in the flesh!

Can anyone in authority take criticism well? They had studied long and hard. They had paid their dues to reach their level of authority. I am only using them as an example most of us are familiar with.

Does this mean we intend to change what the Bible says? Absolutely not! The Bible remains our authority and not individuals. Truth never changes. Sure, it is difficult for anyone to set aside what they believe even for a moment to consider another view. For anyone to change their mind, they must first admit they may be wrong. For some, that is almost impossible to do. The book of Acts gives us an example of some people who are referred to as being "more noble." They are called Bereans because they were from Berea. Acts 17:11:

> 11 **These were more** noble **than those in Thessalonica, in that** <u>they received the word with all readiness of mind, and searched the scriptures daily, whether those things were so.</u>

There it is. To be noble, we must be willing to be open to listening. Then, we must check the Scriptures to see if what was said is so. This should apply to every Christian believer who listens to preaching and teaching about the Bible. If we do that, then we make Scripture the authority! It is the Scripture which was, is, and will always be the Authority. Jesus Christ is the Word of God!

Friend, I did what I am asking you to do. While going through my Master of Biblical Studies, I listened to a conservative Baptist pastor with a doctorate preach at a country church. This was a treat and I eagerly listened. As I listened, I realized that what the pastor said conflicted with other parts of the Bible. It was this moment of conflict that started by search for a system to correctly interpret the Bible. If this book creates a conflict for you, then that created an opportunity for you to examine what you believe. I say that "with conflict comes resolution." It was perfect timing in my life to test everything I was taught. In my post-doctoral studies, I researched and wrote a book called *Letters To Theophilus.* The word "Theophilus" means "one who loves God." It was written as an academic textbook. This present book *The Hidden Gospel* has must of the same information but, as requested, I made it more easy to understand.

I wrote my dissertation on this research. Some years later, the president of the seminary called me. He had reread my dissertation and asked if I still believed that what I wrote was the truth. In response, I told him that I had tested it for two years since graduation. Based upon that testing, I am convinced it is true. This information is what I am presenting to you. Independent study is common for many post graduate programs. In both insurance and the seminary classes, I had learned enough to recognize a contradiction. The Word of God is perfect. Therefore, any error in God-s Word must be from man's interpretation. All of us have listened to and read what men teach. We must always compare this to the Bible. A bookcase will not tell us what to read or who we should listen to. God gives us the freedom of choice. We each have the gift of free will. What a bookcase can do is organize our thoughts and our beliefs. So, as we move forward, we are going to build a sturdy bookcase together.

I would like to share a personal experience. In my early seminary years, I found what I call my Study-Buddy. He was and is my constant companion. We would rejoice in the new things I learned. Those things I didn't understand, I would ask Him to explain them to me. It is the Holy Spirit Who actually does the teaching of God's Word. Scripture was created by the Holy Spirit in a process called "inspiration." The way man can understand Scripture comes from the Holy Spirit also. This process is called "illumination." He is, unquestionably, the "light unto our path" of understanding. I strongly encourage you that in your studies you trust Him to teach you. Ask Him for the answer. However, when we ask God for something, there are two things we must do. First, we must be patient and wait in expectation for His answer. Second, we must look for the answer or we will miss it. Again, wait for the answer and, in faith, be looking for it! The Holy Spirit wants us to understand His Word! He was with me as a student and with me now as I write and teach. The Spirit wants to be our Guide and Companion; our Helper and Comforter. All we have to do is ask Him.

This book is an introduction. Once you have finished it, you should have a solid foundation. You will understand the framework of Bible. You will be confident about your salvation. You will understand that the end times are not to be feared, but looked forward to in hope. Once we understand God's plan, everything that is going on now, will suddenly make sense to you. Why? Because you are seeing it from God's perspective.

Friend, it may sound like we are biting off a lot to chew. This is a relatively short book. There is an old saying that to eat an elephant, you eat it one bite at a time. God spoke through the prophet Isaiah and tells us how He will teach the people. Isaiah 28:9-10:

> **9 Whom shall he teach knowledge? and whom shall he make to understand doctrine? them that are weaned from the milk, and drawn from the breasts.**
>
> **10 For precept must be upon precept, precept upon precept;**

**line upon line, line upon line;
here a little, and there a little:**

God teaches each of us a little bit at a time. Each piece of understanding is built upon another. Those who continually learn from His Word will be rewarded. I have very good news for you. Once you understand the framework, you will be surprised how fast this can happen!

This framework, like a bookcase, organizes everything and holds it all together. There is another word for framework. In seminary, we called it a "system." What you are learning is a "system" of interpretation that will make life so much easier. A "system" is a tool. It is not a religion. There is no church affiliation to join. It is perspective! As you read this book, think about what is presented. I urge you to invite the Holy Spirit to be your "Study-Buddy." I only present the information with the hope that people will read, understand, and enjoy their Bible. Now, relax and enjoy the tour!

3

How Firm A Foundation

I chose the chapter title from a hymn of the same name. Its first two lines are, "How firm a foundation, ye saints of the Lord, Is laid for your faith in His excellent Word!" Before anyone can construct a building they need to look at the blueprints to see its general layout. Looking at the blueprint, we can see the arrangement of the walls that divide the different rooms. God is the Architect. He designed the Bible. By looking at the blueprint of the Bible, we will begin to see God's ultimate plan. He knew its design before the earth was even created. God knew in advance that Adam would sin and the need for a solution. By understanding the blueprint, we will have the solid foundation upon which we can build.

I used two images: a bookcase and a foundation. The concept of organizing something remains the same. Often, we know things, but our thoughts or the facts are unorganized. When it comes to the

Bible, many people feel overwhelmed with all the information. Some may feel this is like a heap of books piled high in their mind. This includes books they read, sermons they listened to, and Bible studies they countless endured. They need something to help them organize all of this. If we want to move freely around the Bible like we were walking about a vast museum, then the blueprint would help us. We are about to solve this problem. We will introduce the "system" that will help us organize our thoughts and information to better understand the whole Bible.

Not only will it organize our information, it will also help us to recall that information. Why? It is because we know where the information is stored. Think about our imaginary bookcase. There are seven shelves and the information is on the sixth shelf. Remember, this "system" doesn't change any of the information! Nothing in the Bible will be changed. It's a simple-to-learn way to store and provide quicker access to that knowledge. For those people who already have their thoughts organized, that is wonderful. We are going to build a new bookcase with empty shelves. At your own pace, you can move your information into the new bookcase after you have tested it. I did and I survived. Now, I am reaping the benefits. I love the Bible. I enjoy reading it and, now, teaching it to others!

Whether you are a beginner or a seasoned theologian, this new bookcase or framework will organize your thoughts differently. Once again, it does not change the content of the Bible. If we sort a list of items by name or by price, it doesn't change the content of the list. It simply changes the order and, in our case, it changes the perspective. I want to encourage everyone who is eager to understand the Bible. Some may have tried to read the entire Bible from cover to cover in one year. It is about the size of the novel *War and Peace*. Consider the Old Testament. The Jews call their Scripture the Tanakh. This is an acronym for its three parts: The Law, The Prophets, and The Writings. They divided it into three sections. You can't sit down and read the Bible from cover to cover. It wasn't arranged that way. To those who have tried, it won't make sense because it is not a novel. We need a simple approach to fully understand the Bible . . . the way God wanted it understood.

Friend, I have really good news! We are going to make it so much easier. I promise you that, if you bear with me a while, you will understand the framework of the Bible. Consider me as your tour guide. However, since our space is limited, this tour will only stop at important sites where we present the defining moment. Once you understand the "system," you can go back and test the system yourself.

Remember, a "system" is like a carpenter's measuring tape or level. It is nothing more than a tool. Where did this "system" come from? It came from instructions given by the Apostle Paul to a ministry trainee. Paul wrote letters to Timothy and Titus who were in training to become pastors. No student of the Bible wants to be embarrassed or "ashamed" by incorrectly interpreting Scripture. Here is Paul's instruction in 2 Timothy 2:15:

15 Study to shew thyself approved unto God, a workman that needeth not to be ashamed, rightly dividing the word of truth.

The Greek word translated "rightly dividing" literally means "cutting with great precision." You might ask, "Isn't that what surgeons do?" Exactly! We are going to carefully cut or divide the Bible into sections. These sections will make sense as God works towards His ultimate purpose. Paul instructed Timothy to "rightly divide" the Word of Truth. This is going to be our approach to create the framework or "system."

God's purpose and messages become clearer when they are separated using this system. In *Letters*, it goes into great detail explaining the three systems used by evangelical Christians to interpret the Bible.

An evangelical is someone who holds the Bible as inspired, without error, and complete. It is the authority for all believers. These three systems are the one reason why there are so many different Christian churches. In Letters, these three "systems" are examined and tested by using what I call "the test of truth." Any system must: (1) be applied consistently to the entire Bible from Genesis to Revelation and (2) have no contradictions with any other part of the Bible. If it does, then the system has failed.

Our tool will be the dispensational system. I have tested this system for over ten years. It has not failed me and it makes the Bible simple to understand. Bypassing the explanations and testing presented in *Letters*, we'll jump right into applying the best, clearest, and most practical tool to understanding the Bible. We will divide the Bible into sections. As we do, I will summarize the different sections so they make sense to you. Don't worry. Nothing will be cut out of the Bible. We divide it to better study each section. Each section is called a "Dispensation" or an "Age."

Many Christians have never heard this word used before. The word "dispensation" is used four times in the New Testament. (See 1 Cor. 9:17; Eph. 1:10, 3:2; Co. 1:25.) This word deserves an explanation. We must not confuse it with the Catholic meaning of an indulgence. In the past, when a fee was paid in advance, the Catholic Church would grant an indulgence. This was permission to do something that would otherwise not be allowed. This was one of the reasons Luther protested against the Catholic Church. This has nothing to do with our meaning. For us, the word "dispensation" means "the act of dispensing or administering." God's ultimate plan is the complete restoration of His Creation. A "dispensation" may be temporary and be for a short period of time or last until the final restoration. So, the time period applicable for each dispensation varies.

Dividing the Bible into "dispensations" allows us to step back for a moment. When we do, we will be able to look at the Bible as a whole. Then, we can look at it from God's perspective as He works His plan. By doing this, we can see His progress towards the total restoration of His Creation. Perhaps, you have never heard of the Bible being divided. Let me ask you this question. How many days did God take to create the earth? He divided Creation into seven days. Now, this may surprise you. Like the number of "days" in the week, God will take seven dispensations or ages to restore His Creation!

God created the heaven and the earth in six days and, then, on the seventh day He rested. Genesis 2:1-3:

> 1 **Thus the heavens and the earth were finished, and all the host of them.** 2 <u>**And on the seventh day God ended his work which he had made; and he rested on the seventh day from all his work which he had made.**</u> 3 **And God blessed the seventh day, and sanctified it: because that in it he had rested from all his work which God created and made.**

As we study the dispensations, we will see by the seventh dispensation God will have fully restored His Creation.

Most people are well aware of the coming Judgment. Yet, most people don't' know that God's ultimate plan is not to judge the world but to restore His Creation! That certainly changes the perspective. Yes, the Bible tells us about the coming Judgment. However, punishment is reserved for those who rebel against God. They are His enemies. They fight against Him. Punishment is for those who choose, by their own free will, to reject Him.

At the time I am writing this book, there is still time. Currently, there is an offer from God on the table. It can either be accepted or rejected by anyone who understands the offer. This book has two objectives. First, I want you to understand the Bible as a whole. Second, I want you to understand what God's current offer is during this present dispensation. Once you understand the offer, you must make your own decision. Like looking at the time clock for a professional ball game, there is a time. However, like that clock, there is a time limit to His offer. When this present dispensation comes to an end, God's gracious offer of salvation by grace through faith alone will be withdrawn. Then, He will move on to finish His plan to restore Creation.

4

Upon This Foundation

We understand this foundation when we can follow the blueprint. This blueprint represents the system we will use. It divides the building or Bible into divisions or sections. Like a foundation, the system must be solid. I must support everything that is built upon it. We can be confident of this because there is only one foundation. The words from another hymn read, "the Church's one foundation is Jesus Christ her Lord." It is the Lord Jesus Christ Who is the Word of God. (See Jn. 1:1-5.)

Previously, I stated the Bible has seven dispensation. Like the Creation and God's Restoration of Creation will take six dispensation or ages to complete. In the seventh Age with Creation restored, God will declare eternal rest. During these seven dispensations, God was, is, and will always be the One Who administers His Creation. God is the head. He manages His household by appointing certain overseers. The Greek word for "dispensation" is a compound word made up of "household" and "law or rule." In other words, a "dispensation" is an "act of managing a household." The manager acts as a "steward." You may recognize the names of some stewards: Adam, Noah, Abraham, and Moses are familiar to most people. Their stories are recorded in Genesis and Exodus and paint a picture of Who God is and how He interacts with those He created.

God made this easy. The first five of the seven dispensations are found in the first two books of the Bible! Everyone should read Genesis and Exodus. If you like stories, you will enjoy these two books. Each book, written in the narrative style, are important to the development of the framework. We are told that God wants everyone to understand. The Bible tells us that God our Saviour desires ". . . all men to be saved, and to come unto the knowledge of the truth" (1 Tim. 2:4). How can they be saved? All can be saved by coming to the knowledge of the Word of God – the Bible! It won't be long before you start to see the big picture.

How are we to cut or divide the Bible into dispensations? We do this by noting changes in the narrative. Governments rule over the affairs of nations. They do this by using different administrators. In the same way, God governs His Creation by dispensing His plans through various administrators. The seven dispensations have different names to help us refer to them. The names are usually connected to its teacher or purpose. These names are assigned only for reference. God's purpose for each dispensation remains unchanged despite its name. Four dispensations are introduced in the book of Genesis. The fifth is introduced in Exodus.

We will summarize of the first five dispensation for two reasons. First, these are not our present dispensation. Second, they provide an historical understanding of the events leading up to the current age as well as the fulfillment of prophecy in the end times. This does not mean that the details are not important. The book *Letters* provides a much broader explanation of each dispensation. It is an excellent follow-up to this book. These summaries help us understand how each of the dispensations relates to God's ultimate plan. Like explorers looking for treasure, we are looking for the hidden gospel in the Bible. Like hidden treasure, it is possible for anyone to find it. However, it is best if they know where to look. Now, we could say that the blueprint is actually a treasure map. How exciting!

Every Sunday, most evangelical churches will preach from the Bible. They offer Bible classes and have Bible conferences. However, most of these churches preach from the Bible topically. That means they concentrate on the specific and not the general. So, their listeners have a collection of Polaroid® snapshots of the Bible without seeing the larger picture. The gospel remains hidden to many Christian teachers. Why? From my personal observation, they teach what they were taught without the benefit of a system to guide them. Paul calls it "foolishness!" That's a rather abrasive accusation. We better take a look at what Paul means by this.

That was an interesting word for him to choose. I want to make it clear that I am not saying that those who preach and teach are foolish. That is certainly not the case. Paul refers those who believed what he taught was foolishness! Let's go to the authority and see what the Bible says about foolishness in the following verses:

1 Corinthians 1:18-25:

> **18 For the preaching of the cross is to them that perish <u>foolishness</u>; but unto us which are saved it is the power of God. 19 For it is written, I will destroy the wisdom of the wise, and will bring**

to nothing the understanding of the prudent.

20 Where is the wise? where is the scribe? where is the disputer of this world? hath not God made <u>foolish</u> the wisdom of this world? 21 For after that in the wisdom of God the world by [its] wisdom knew not God, it pleased God by the <u>foolishness</u> of preaching to save them that believe.

22 For the Jews require a sign, and the Greeks seek after wisdom: 23 But we preach Christ crucified, unto the Jews a stumblingblock, and unto the Greeks <u>foolishness</u>; 24 But unto them which are called, both Jews and Greeks, Christ the power of God, and the wisdom of God. 25 Because the <u>foolishness</u> of God is wiser than men; and the weakness of God is stronger than men.

1 Corinthians 2:13-14:

13 Which things also we speak, not in the words which man's wisdom teacheth, but which the Holy Ghost

teacheth; comparing spiritual things with spiritual. 14 But the natural man receiveth not the things of the Spirit of God: for they are <u>foolishness</u> unto him: neither can he know them, because they are spiritually discerned.

1 Corinthians 3:18-20:

18 Let no man deceive himself. If any man among you seemeth to be wise in this world, let him become a fool, that he may be wise. 19 For the wisdom of this world is <u>foolishness</u> with God. For it is written, He taketh the wise in their own craftiness. 20 And again, The Lord knoweth the thoughts of the wise, that they are vain.

Some very learned teachers and preachers who are greatly respected by men teach the customs and traditions of men. They teach the philosophies of men. It is comfortable for them to stay within their own tradition. Going outside their traditional beliefs would displease their followers. It could result in them losing their job. It is what most Christians want to hear. Teaching something different, even if it is in the Word of God, would upset them. Thus, when presented with the simple truth for this present Age, most people consider it to be "foolishness." If they have never heard it before, then it must not be true. Nothing has changed. This was the same reaction the Pharisees had when confronted by the living Word of God Himself.

Therefore, we must be careful. We must not dismiss Scripture, but let it speak for itself. It is important to reserve judgment until all the evidence has been presented. As we continue, go ahead and search the Scriptures to see if what is being presented is true. Then, ask the Holy Spirit for guidance and then make your decision.

5

Fences

The purpose of fences is to divide or separate something whether to keep something out or keep something in. Fences are not a bad thing. In fact, they serve an important purpose. We need to see divisions in the Bible as fences. We can still look over the fences, but what is inside the fence is generally intended to remain there. The biggest difficulty for some will be to reconsider beliefs, taught and accepted to be true, may be wrong. So, buckle up!

Here it is. All Scripture is written "for" us, but not all Scripture is written "to" us. Those two prepositions make a huge difference in understanding the Bible. If everything is one and the same, then there is no reason for God to create seven different dispensations. Does that make sense? If we make it all one, then the purpose and impact of each dispensation will be lost. The Bible hasn't changed. It is how we see it that needs to change. We can still read the whole Bible to understand Who God is and all His attributes. Paul agrees. 2 Timothy 3:16:

16 All scripture is given by inspiration of God, and is profitable for doctrine, for reproof, for correction, for instruction in righteousness:

Let's use the following story as an example. Over the span of one man's life, he wrote many letters during his ninety years. He wrote to his grandparents as a child and also to his parents while he was away at prep school. He wrote to his girlfriend who would later become his wife. While in the military, his children and grandchildren regularly received sage advice from him because he loved them. He had a distinguished service through WWII. After his death, his great grandchildren published all these letters into a book. Like the Bible, there was only one author and made up of letters written to different family members. All of his letters are true. They can help others to better know him as a man. However, what he wrote to his beloved fiancée were written to her alone. The promises he made to one recipient were not necessarily made to all the others. It is this concept that we need to apply to the Bible.

The Age of Innocence

The Bible opens with Adam and Eve being created in God's image. Later, using their free will, they chose not to believe God. They chose to disobey His instruction. God gave them a warning and made the consequences clear. They did not believe God and, by not believing Him, they showed their lack of faith in God's Word. Satan convinced them that they could be like God. They ate the forbidden fruit from the Tree of Knowledge of Good and Evil. In sinning against God, their eyes were opened. They were no longer perfect and God could not allow them to remain in the Garden of Eden. So, they were evicted.

This first dispensation is called the "Age of Innocence." It began without sin or the knowledge of it. It ends when God sends Adam and Eve out of the garden and into a fallen world. Genesis 3:22-24:

> 22 **And the LORD God said, Behold, the man is become as one of us, to know good and evil: and now, lest he put forth his hand, and take also of the tree of life, and eat, and live for ever:**
>
> 23 **Therefore the LORD God sent him forth from the garden of Eden, to till the ground from whence he was taken.** 24 **So he drove out the man; and he placed at the east of the garden of Eden**

Cherubims, and a flaming sword which turned every way, to keep the way of the tree of life.

Dispensations have no set time period. The Age of Innocence ended with Adam and Eve being driven from the Garden of Eden. They were prevented from returning and entered into a different world.

This dispensation had a lasting impact. It is because of Adam's sin that all mankind are guilty. All mankind will die because of Adam's sin. Sin is passed from father to child in each generation. It is for that reason that Christ's Father must be God. It was the Holy Spirit Who caused Mary to be with child. We read in 1 Corinthians 15:22:

22 For as in Adam all die, even so in Christ shall all be made alive.

Adam's sin is called the "original sin." The curse upon Adam applies to all mankind. This problem would remain unless God provided a Solution.

Age of Conscience

When the first couple left the Garden of Eden, God made coverings for them from animal skins. It is said this was the first sacrifice providing a "temporary covering." God instilled a conscience in them and in all their future children. The "conscience" is often called the Moral Law. Every person is born with this internal guide between right and wrong. This became the basis by which people came to judge each other. Later, we will see in the Gospels that Christ warns people not to judge others. Matthew 7:1-2:

> 1 **Judge not, that ye be not judged.** 2 **For with what judgment ye judge, ye shall be judged: and with what measure ye mete, it shall be measured to you again.**

I was having a conversation with an atheist who thought it was unfair for God to judge those who "were not saved." I told him that God wouldn't need to. They will be condemned by their own judgement of others who do the same things they do. The conscience was intended to be a powerful guide.

The first murder happened when Cain killed his brother Abel. As the children of Adam and Eve multiplied, they became more and more sinful. Finally, it reached a point where God could no longer look upon the world's sin. He would judge the earth by a Flood. Noah was the first evangelist. Note the many similarities to the present-day. Noah warned people of the coming judgment. Of the millions of inhabitants on earth, only eight were saved in the Ark because they believed. Noah, his three sons, and their wives had faith in God and that saved them. The Flood covered the earth and killed all who chose not to believe. However, those who believed and entered the safety of the Ark were saved.

God offers salvation, but everyone has free will and can choose to accept or reject His offer. Later, in the Gospels, Jesus compares the days of Noah to the end times and the coming of the Kingdom. Matthew 24:37-39

37 **But as the days of Noe [Noah] were, so shall also the coming of the Son of man be.**

38 **For as in the days that were before the flood they were eating and drinking, marrying and giving in marriage, until the day that Noe [Noah] entered into the ark, 39 And knew not until the flood came, and took them all away; so shall also the coming of the Son of man be.**

The Ark finally came to rest on solid ground. Noah and his family left the Ark. This ends the second dispensation since, like Adam and Eve, they couldn't go back to the way the world was before the Flood. Unable to return, they must move on with their consciences as their guide. God gave these survivors instructions. Genesis 9:1:

> 1 **And God blessed Noah and his sons, and said unto them, Be fruitful, and multiply, and replenish the earth.**

The word "replenish" means "refill." They were to multiply and refill the earth again. However, we will see that this is not what Noah's descendants did.

Age of Human Government

Instead of following God's direction to refill and cover the earth, they came together and created the first city called Babel. We get our word "babble" from this. When someone is talking and we can't understand them, it is often said they are babbling. Much happened in this dispensation. It will have a major impact on human events and will be evident in the end times. This dispensation established human government. They hold the power of capital punishment or the right to condemn someone to death. The sins of mankind can't be contained. They became drunk with power. Government by humans will continue to grow into what we see in world governments today.

From this historical record we learn the origin of languages and the nations. Genesis 11:4-9:

> 4 And they said, Go to, let us build us a city and a tower, whose top may reach unto heaven; and let us make us a name, lest we be scattered abroad upon the face of the whole earth. 5 And the LORD came down to see the city and the tower, which the children of men builded.
>
> 6 And the LORD said, Behold, the people is one, and they have all one language; and this they begin to do: and now nothing will be restrained from them, which they have imagined to do.
>
> 7 Go to, let us go down, and there confound their language, that they may not understand one another's speech. 8 So the LORD scattered them abroad from thence upon the face of all the earth: and they left off to build the city.
>
> 9 Therefore is the name of it called Babel; because the LORD did there confound the language of all the earth: and from thence did the LORD scatter them abroad upon the face of all the earth.

The people came together and collectively built the Tower of Babel. This coming together edified the efforts and combined power of man which is much like what we see in global government today. Their collective efforts built a tower into the heavens. They chose astrology as their god and not God the Creator. No longer were they interested in glorifying God. Their past actions mirror what we see today. Presently, mankind is working its way back to a combined one-world government without God. To delay this happening so soon, God scattered the people and confused their languages. This is how God divided the people of the world into nations.

This great sum of the people will be referred to in the Bible by three names: the Nations, the Gentiles, the Heathen which are people "without God." Later, once God creates Israel, they will also be called non-Jews or the Uncircumcision. Whatever they are called, you now know their origin. Collectively, they chose to turn away from God. In the end times, it will be these Nations who battle with God as they attempt to annihilate God's people Israel. At this point, there is no Israel. There are only the nations which have now been divided by their tribes and languages.

6

The Seed

There is much confusion among Christians concerning the word "church." For this reason, I personally don't often use the word, but instead choose to use the word "assembly." The misunderstanding stems from the misuse of the word "church" which means "the called-out ones." In other words, they are a unique subset of a larger group. When Christ uses the word in the New Testament, He is referring to the "calling out" of believing Jews from among the larger group of who don't believe. In this chapter, we will look at the individual Abraham who was "called out" from among the Nations. There are Christians who reason that this was the beginning of "the Church." The evidence will prove this claim is false.

The first dispensation began with Adam. From it, we learned the origin of sin and death which affects all mankind. In the second dispensation, we learned the origin of the conscience which was to be man's internal guide to right and wrong. In the last dispensation, we looked at a collective group who rebelled against God and turned away from following Him. God divided this rebellious people into smaller tribes or nations. However, they all remain part of the whole referred to as "The Nations."

In this next dispensation, we find God "calls out" one man from the nations because of his faith. This one man would become the father of a great nation. God separates them from the others nations for a specific purpose. God has His ultimate plan. By choosing this man of faith, God will create a nation for Himself. This holy nation will play a key role in His plans to restore Creation.

Age of Promise

We are going to look at the promise God made to Abraham. When God makes an agreement with someone, it is called a "covenant." This particular agreement will be the "Abrahamic Covenant." Covenants made by God are permanent and can't be changed. We will look at some covenants that are "conditional" and others are "unconditional." A condition is an "if-then" clause. Here is an example. "If you pay me the money, then I will sell you my house." The person is only obligated to fulfill his promise if the condition is met. If the payment is made, then the house will be sold. In the same way, if the condition is not met, the house will not be sold. The idea of conditions in agreements is important. However, the *Abrahamic Covenant* is unconditional because God Himself will fulfill the agreement regardless of the actions of the other party. In other words, God Himself guaranties its fulfillment.

Let's look at God's unconditional promise to Abraham. Genesis 12:1-3:

> 1 **Now the LORD had said unto Abram, Get thee out of thy country, and from thy kindred, and from thy father's house, unto a land that I will shew thee:**
>
> 2 **And I will make of thee a great nation, and I will bless thee, and make thy name great; and thou shalt be a blessing:**
>
> 3 **And I will bless them that bless thee, and curse him that curseth thee: and in thee shall all families of the earth be blessed.**

This is only the beginning of the promises God will make to Abraham. Genesis 15:5-6:

5 And he [God] brought him [Abraham] forth abroad, and said, Look now toward heaven, and tell the stars, if thou be able to number them: and he [God] said unto him [Abraham], So shall thy seed be.

6 **And he [Abraham] believed in the LORD; and he [God] counted it to him [Abraham] for righteousness.**

What made Abraham so special? Simply, he believed God! Believing in God's Word is "faith!" Abraham was a righteous man according to God. Why? He believed God!. The above Scripture is critical. You must remember the importance of faith in obtaining righteousness and, therefore, salvation!

Everything in the Bible relates to God's restoration of Creation. The Abrahamic Covenant was made with Abraham, but it also included Abraham's Seed. Here is another important point. The word "seed" can be either singular or plural. It could be one seed of grass or it can be a whole bag of grass seed. Don't miss this point! God is using the word "seed" to refer to a Person and not a people! That's right. Abraham's Seed is one singular, very special person. What Paul wrote in the New Testament confirms this. Galatians 3:16:

16 **Now to Abraham and his seed were the promises made**. He saith not, And to seeds, as of many; but as of one, <u>And to thy seed, which is Christ</u>.

Who is this Seed? The above verse tells us. The Seed is the Lord Jesus Christ Who is a direct descendent of Abraham!

The New Testament records Jesus' ancestors in the same way England records the rightful heirs to the throne. We find our proof in the very first verse of the very first book in the New Testament. Matthew 1:1:

1 **The book of the generation of <u>Jesus Christ</u>, the son of David, <u>the son of Abraham</u>**.

The blessings and promises that God gave to Abraham belong to him and will be fulfilled in Jesus Christ, the Son of Abraham, the Son of God.

During this Age of Promise, another promise is given to King David. You can see from the above verse that Jesus is also the Son of David. Let's take a look at the promise God made to David called the "Davidic Covenant." God begins by telling David what will follow after his death concerning the future of his kingdom. When you see the word "seed" used the following verses, you already know Who the Seed is. 1 Chronicles 17:11:

> 11 **And it shall come to pass, when thy days be expired that thou must go to be with thy fathers, that I will raise up <u>thy seed</u> after thee, which shall be of thy sons; and <u>I [God] will establish his [the Seed's] kingdom.</u>**

It continues by stating what the Seed of David will accomplish. Verses 12-14:

> 12 **He shall build me an house, and <u>I will stablish his throne for ever.</u> 13 <u>I will be his father, and he shall be my son</u>: and I will not take my mercy away from him, as I took it from him [King Saul] that was before thee:**

> 14 **But <u>I will settle him in mine house and in my kingdom for ever: and his throne shall be established for evermore.</u>**

This singular Seed will be the eternal King in God's eternal Kingdom.

Jesus Christ is the Seed! He is the heir to the promises God made to Abraham. He will be heir to King David's throne and reign forever. The Jews knew their Scripture. Therefore, they knew what it meant when the Anointed One or the Messiah appeared. It was for this reason they called Jesus Christ throughout the Gospels "the Son of David." Later, in the book of Revelation, we will see that Jesus Christ is anointed as the King Who will reign forever! How does the dispensation called the Age of Promise play into God's ultimate plan? God "called out" a people from among the Nations for a purpose. God is not finished with the children of Abraham. We will find out God's purpose for the children of Abraham in the next chapter.

Although time moves on, God's promises and covenants can't change. The Word of God remains forever.

7

A Peculiar People

When we think about Israel, we must think of them from the same perspective as God sees them. They are a family. They are "the children of Abraham." In AD 70, Jerusalem was completely destroyed and uninhabitable. That destruction occurred forty years after the Crucifixion. Not until 1948 was there a declaration which created the State of Israel. The geopolitical entity is known as Medinat Yisra'el or the State of Israel. It is a democracy created by man. Since their first king, Saul, Israel has been a theocracy with a monarch or king as God's representative.

Unlike those saved by grace through believing God, Israel's faith must be tested. That is the distinguishing factor and we will see it again later. Their salvation will be based, like their father Abraham, upon their faith and their lineage. That lineage began with Abraham who had a son named Isaac. He had a son whose name was Jacob. God changed Jacob's name to Israel and he had sons also. One of his sons was named Joseph. We find the story of Jospeh towards the end of Genesis. (See Gen. 30:22-50:26.) Joseph is a type or foreshadowing of the Savior Who would save His people Israel.

This is how the nation of Israel came to be. There was a great famine and all of Jacob's family had come to Egypt for food. They remained in Egypt under Joseph, Jacob's son, who ruled on behalf of the Pharoah. The family prospered there and grew into a large people. As time went on, Joseph died. The Pharoah who had blessed Joseph also died. Exodus 1:8:

8 Now there arose up a new king over Egypt, which knew not Joseph.

This new Pharoah saw how powerful the children of Abraham had become. He sought to subdue them and made them slaves. You should read both Genesis and Exodus. They tell historical stories and are easy to read. Now, the children of Abraham found themselves under a tyrannical king and they needed to be saved. Who could God send?

Born into the family of Abraham and educated in the household of Pharoah, was a man named

Moses. God chose him to lead the children of Abraham out of this Egyptian bondage. Not willing to let them go, God needed to reveal His power through curses. One such curse would kill all firstborn which included Pharoah's own son. God had instructed Moses in advance to have the Jews mark their doorways with the blood of a lamb. If they believed and obeyed God, then He would "pass over" that home. No one in that house would die because the blood of the lamb would protect them. Every year the children of Abraham remember this event called "the Passover."

It makes sense now when we read that John the Baptist proclaimed that Jesus Christ is the Lamb of God. John 1:29:

> 29 **The next day John seeth Jesus coming unto him, and saith, <u>Behold the Lamb of God</u>, which taketh away the sin of the world.**

Their Messiah is the Passover Lamb. Remember the Last Supper and twelve men sitting at a table with the Son of God. They were celebrating Passover with the Lamb of God Himself! The very next day this Lamb of God was slain. This all took place as prophesied and recorded for us in the Word of God.

God chose Moses to free His people. He would lead them to the Promise Land which is something else God promised to Abraham and his Seed. During their sojourn in the Wilderness, God wanted to teach the children of Israel to be totally dependent upon Him. However, they were a proud people and determined to do things their own way. So, if they wouldn't learn the lesson willingly, then God would spell it out for them contractually. He gave them the "Mosaic Covenant." Think of it as a very detailed list or do's and don'ts. If they wanted to do it themselves, then this is what they needed to do.

The Mosaic Covenant is conditional with the results depending upon how Israel honors the covenant agreement. If they keep the agreement, then God will bless them. If they failed to keep every single requirement, then God will punish them. This is called "the blessings and the curses" in the Mosaic Covenant. Remember, all conditional covenants have "if-then" conditions. Deuteronomy 11:26-28:

> 26 Behold, <u>I set before you this day a blessing and a curse;</u> 27 <u>A blessing, if ye obey</u> the commandments of the LORD your God, which I command you this day: 28 <u>And a curse, if ye will not obey</u> the commandments of the LORD your God . . .

God made this covenant with Israel alone. This covenant can't be transferred or assigned to some other party no matter how loud they yell. As a result, the children of Abraham became Israel – a separate nation under God. There are 613 commandments in the Mosaic Covenant which are binding upon the Jews. Later, when you see in the New Testament references to "bondage to the Law" or "the weight of the Law," you will understand why.

The Age of Law

This is the fifth age or dispensation. You saw that the Mosaic Covenant is conditional! God also created the Levitical Priesthood to deal with the sins of the people temporarily. The priests would intercede for those who broke the Mosaic Law. Various sacrifices were designated depending on the severity of the sin. However, these sacrifices would only "cover" the sin and not remove it. Like the animal skins God provided for Adam and Eve, their "covering" was only temporary. The people needed to know that there is a cost to sin. They paid for these animal sacrifices to "cover" their sin. Later, all the sins of believing Israel will be forgiven by the Messiah when He returns. We will discuss His return later in this book.

It is important for you to see this. In order for the covenant to be a "binding agreement," all the children of Israel must willingly commit to the agreement! As with any agreement, both parties must agree. Below is the ratification of the agreement by both parties. The children of Abraham approved or confirmed the covenant as presented to them by Moses. The confirmation of their acceptance was returned to God. This made it a binding agreement. Exodus 19:1-6:

1 In the third month, when <u>the children of Israel</u> were gone forth out of the land of Egypt, the same day came they into the wilderness of Sinai. 2 For they were departed from Rephidim, and were come to the desert of Sinai, and had pitched in the wilderness; and there Israel camped before the mount.

3 And Moses went up unto God, and the LORD called unto him out of the mountain, saying, <u>Thus shalt thou say to the house of Jacob, and tell the children of Israel;</u>

4 Ye have seen what I did unto the Egyptians, and how I bare you on eagles' wings, and brought you unto myself.

5 <u>Now therefore, if ye will obey my voice indeed, and keep my covenant, then ye shall be a peculiar treasure unto me above all people</u>: for all the earth is mine:

6 And ye shall be unto me <u>a kingdom of priests</u>, and <u>an holy nation</u>. These are the words which thou shalt speak unto the children of Israel.

Everything so far in the Bible is working towards the achievement of God's plan to restore Creation. Look at verse 5 above. The word "peculiar" does not mean off. It means "individually unique." What does this mean?

Israel is to be different or unique from all other nations. They are to be a "holy" nation. Here, the word "holy" means "separated from the other nations" and "belonging to God." They are to be God's treasure. The role of Israel in the future kingdom will be as a priesthood. We will see this in the book of Revelation. The other nations who remain after the great judgment will go through Israel, as priests, in order to interact with God. Israel will stand between God and the nations once the eternal kingdom is established. We are speaking about an earthly kingdom with Jerusalem at its center. There are many prophecies about this. Consider Zechariah 8:23:

> 23 **Thus saith the LORD of hosts; In those days it shall come to pass, that ten men shall take hold out of all languages of the nations, even shall take hold of the skirt of him that is a Jew, saying, <u>We will go with you: for we have heard that God is with you.</u>**

In the restored earth, the other nations will seek out the Jews so that they may go with them to worship God the Creator. For the Jews will be the priesthood for God.

For the Jews, the Dispensation of Law is still in effect. Nothing has changed for them. When the Messiah came, we are told He came to fulfill the promises made to their fathers: Abraham, Isaac, and Jacob. Paul tells us this in Romans 15:8:

> 8 **Now I say that Jesus Christ was <u>a minister of the circumcision</u> for the truth of God, <u>to confirm the promises made unto the fathers</u>:**

Here, the Jews are called the "circumcision" which was a physical mark of the Abrahamic Covenant. Therefore, Paul says the Messiah was specifically sent to confirm or fulfill the promises that God made to Abraham, Isaac, and Jacob! They are the fathers that Paul is referring to.

Concerning the Mosaic Law, look at what Jesus said to them during His earthly ministry. Matthew 5:17:

> 17 **Think not that I am come to destroy the law, or the prophets: I am not come to destroy, but [rather] to fulfil.**

Jesus Christ came both to "fulfill" the Law as well as to "**confirm the promises made unto the fathers.**" I didn't want you to miss that important point. Christ did this for the Jews. They are the ones called the "circumcision." Be patient. We are only in the fifth age, the Age of Law. We have not gotten to the Gentile yet. Later, we will find out how this applies to the Gentiles who are the "uncircumcision." This may be different from what you have been taught. The facts are important. It will all make sense to you soon!

The weight of the Law is oppressive. It was designed that way. Sometimes it is referred to as being in "bondage" under the Law. God is teaching the

Jews, or the "circumcision," a valuable lesson. They must be totally dependent upon Him. James, one of the Twelve, wrote the book of James to the Jews. He began his letter, "to the twelve tribes which are scattered abroad" (Jas. 1:1). Later, he explains the weight of the Law in James 2:10:

> 10 **For whosoever shall keep the whole law, and yet offend [break] in one point, he is guilty of all.**

Notice what James says! If one keeps the whole Law but breaks one point of the Law, then he has broken them all! They either got one-hundred percent right or they failed the test. Talk about stress or a burden! No wonder it's call "bondage" under the Law.

By willingly accepting the Mosaic Covenant, Israel became obligated to keep the entire Mosaic Law. The Jews have always struggled with faith – believing God. Even though God had miraculously saved them from Egypt, their lack of faith persisted in the Wilderness. We find that it was lack of faith that prevented them from entering the Promised Land. It is not a great distance between Egypt and the land promised to Abraham. Why did God cause them to wander in the Wilderness for forty years? There is the simple answer. It was their lack of faith! (See Num. 13:1-14:39.)

Later, we are told by the Apostle Paul that the Law was to be their schoolmaster. Its purpose is to teach Israel to be depend upon God – to have "faith" in Him. Galatians 3:24-25:

> 24 **Wherefore the law <u>was our school-master</u> to bring us unto Christ, that we might be justified by faith.** 25 **<u>But after that faith is come, we are no longer under a schoolmaster.</u>**

Their forty years in the Wilderness were to teach Israel to depend upon God for everything like food, water, and protection. Their father Abraham believed and, by believing God, his faith was counted to him as righteousness.

Israel remains self-sufficient and self-determined like a willful child instead of depending upon God. The Law was to reveal their constant need for God. Israel's only hope will be complete dependence upon God and faith in what God has already told them. It is their faith in the Word of God that will save them!

8

An Interruption

A lot of people look around at world events and wonder about the end times. When you have finished reading this book you will have a good knowledge of God's plan. You will have a clearer biblical understanding as to where we are now and what lays ahead. There are powers, principalities, and rulers of darkness who try prevent people from understanding the Word of God. We have the Comforter Who is the Spirit of God. He illuminates God's Word for those who seek Him.

At the beginning of this book, you were told there are seven dispensation. There are. However, most teachers were taught that these seven dispensations are sequential. They are not! This means that the series starts with one and goes straight to seven like chapters numbered in a book. This is not the case! There is an interruption to the series! Here is where we part company with many in the crowd. However, it is this very difference that is critical to to understanding the Bible!

Most teachers and preachers who have learned "rightly dividing the Word of Truth" were taught that the next dispensation follows the Age of Law. We will see, in a moment, this causes conflicts with prophecy. We are not going to get too deep into theology. In fact, the difference is very simple. There is an interruption to the Age of Law. The rulers of Israel rejected their Messiah. Not only did they reject Him, but they crucified Him. You can understand how this could cause a temporary suspension in the Age of Law which will resume to it completion according to God's promises. Don't worry. This will all make sense when we are finished with the explanation!

The above statement is against what most people have been taught. I spoke with one preacher who said they were "aware of the conflicts" in what they were taught. He went on to say that they were willing to continue believing what they were taught "holding those conflicts in tension" until the Lord returns. So, they will overlook these conflicts, but continue to teach the same theology. Friend, we must turn away from the knowledge of man! We must instead turn to God's wisdom which is His Word. We will now look at a prophecy that establishes a time-line. I was teaching a class on Revelation and began by asking the students to turn to the book of Daniel. This is important. The key to understanding Revelation is the prophet Daniel. My books *The Glorious Destiny of Israel* and *Letters to Theophilus* go into greater detail than we can here. This book is only a summary. It introduces a system of interpreting the Bible of which few people are aware.

After leaving Egypt, Israel wandered in the Wilderness for forty years and finally entered the Promised Land about 1406 BC. They continually broke the Mosaic Law which resulted in punishment. The ten northern tribes, called Israel, were eventually assimilated into other cultures following their defeat to the Assyrians. The two remaining tribes, Benjamin and Judah, were taken into exile in Babylon. They remained there for seventy years. Jerusalem remained desolate and fell into decay. The Prophet Daniel was one of the princes of Judah taken to Babylon. Daniel was concerned about what the other nations would think when they saw the state of Jerusalem. He prayed to God asking Him when He would restore His Holy City. God sent an angel, but the response far exceeded Daniel's expectations.

Jerusalem would be restored as God's Holy City. It would become home to His eternal Kingdom ruled by the eternal King! Let's break down Daniel's prophecy into bite-size pieces. The brackets are added for clarification. Daniel 9:24:

> 24 **Seventy weeks are determined upon thy people and upon thy holy city, to [1] finish the transgression, and [2] to make an end of sins, and [3] to make reconciliation for iniquity, and [4] to bring in everlasting righteousness, and [5] to seal up the vision and prophecy, and [6] to anoint the most Holy.**

Daniel was told that, at the end of this seventy weeks, God will accomplish the six items numbered above. These will complete God's plan to restore His Creation. God will: (1) end sin, (2) make payment for sin, (3) reconcile creation to Himself, (4) establish everlasting righteousness, (5) fulfill the promises and prophecies, and (6) anoint the most Holy One. This is the Lord Jesus Christ, the King of kings and Lord of lords. God's ultimate plan for complete restoration of Creation will be complete!

There is something that I need to clarify before we go on. In this prophecy, each day of the week represents one year. Therefore, one week would be seven years. Seventy weeks would be 490 years. This is a valuable timeline for understanding the end times. Later on, you may want to consider additional reading. I recommend Sir Robert Anderson's *The Coming Prince: The Marvelous Prophecy of Daniel's Seventy Weeks Concerning the Antichrist*. Both *Letters To Theophilus* and *The Glorious Destiny of Israel* are excellent as well.

Now, let us continue with the prophecy. The angel is going to break it down for us. This will be very interesting as it explains so much. Verse 25:

> 25 **Know therefore and understand, that from the going forth of the commandment to restore and to build Jerusalem unto the Messiah the Prince shall be <u>seven weeks, and threescore and two weeks</u>: the street shall be built again, and the wall, even in troublous times.**

Let us do some simple addition. Add seven plus three score which is sixty. Then, add two. The sum is sixty-nine weeks. Then, multiply sixty-nine by seven. We get 483 years. The next verse restates it, but do not forget to include the seven years from verse 25 to equal the sixty-nine weeks. Verse 26:

26 [1] And after threescore and two weeks <u>shall Messiah be cut off</u>, but not for himself: and [2] <u>the people of the prince that shall come shall destroy the city</u> and the sanctuary; and the end thereof shall be with a flood [of people], and unto the end of the war desolations are determined.

Archaeologists have dated the command "to restore and to build Jerusalem" to 453 BC. If we subtract 483 years, then we get a negative thirty. The difference would be the date of 30 AD when the Messiah was cut off. The words "the people of the prince" are followers of the prince or the Antichrist. The angel speaks about a "flood" which is a "flood of people" so numerous that they appear as water. This is the remaining seven years and it will continue "unto the end." (See Matthew 24.)

This prince will make a covenant or agreement with many nations at the beginning of the seven years. Verse 27:

27 And he [the prince] shall confirm the covenant with many for one week [seven years]: and in the midst of the week he shall cause the sacrifice and the oblation [non-blood offerings] to cease,

**and for the overspreading of abomina-
tions he shall make it desolate, even until the consummation [the completion
or end], and that [which is] determined
shall be poured upon the desolate.**

In the middle of these seven years, the Antichrist will break the covenant he made. In Revelation, this midpoint is referred to as three and one-half
years, forty-two months, or 1,260 days. They are the
same. From the midpoint, the remaining time that
following will be considered the Great Tribulation.
Consider the words of Jesus Christ concerning this
time. Matthew 24:22:

22 **And except those days should be
shortened, there should no flesh be
saved: but for the elect's [Israel's] sake
those days shall be shortened.**

The reply Daniel received from God answered
far more than his question. He asked God when He
would restore fallen Jerusalem and, now, we have a
timeline. This timeline began at the decree "to restore
and to build Jerusalem" which has been accurately
dated to 453 BC. We know that 483 years into this
timeline, the Messiah will be cut off for a while. If we
add 483 years to 453 BC, we come to 30 AD. Interesting! This would date the crucifixion to 30 AD. Forty

years after His crucifixion, the City of Jerusalem was destroyed in 70 AD. So, what happened?

The timeline began some 2500 years ago. This prophecy should have been fulfilled a long time ago. God knew the Jews would reject their Messiah. However, He did not change the timeline. Nothing changed. The seven remaining years are currently being held in abeyance – in temporary suspension. In the next chapter, we will take a deeper look at this and answer the question, "Why?"

9

Twelve To One

Moving into the New Testament, we find Jesus choosing the Twelve. He would be with them for three years and teach them Himself. To whom does Jesus send His Twelve? Matthew 10:5-6:

> 5 **These twelve Jesus sent forth, and commanded them, saying, <u>Go not into the way of the Gentiles</u>, and into any city of the Samaritans enter ye not: 6 <u>But go rather to the lost sheep of the house of Israel</u>.**

Church tradition teaches that "the Church" started with the Twelve. I disagree, but I am not going to address that at this point. We are in hot pursuit of the answer to the question, "What caused the temporary suspension?" And, here's another good question, "When did this happen?"

It has to do with Stephen who was the first martyr. He was falsely accused of blaspheme and forced to appear before the rulers of Israel. In his speech, recorded in Acts 7:1-53, he accused the rulers of continually rebelling against God. He concludes by charging them with crucifying Israel's Messiah. These rulers were filled with rage, took Stephen outside, and stoned him to death. Now, think back. Do you remember the one sin that would not be forgiven Israel? It was blasphemy against the Holy Spirit. Matthew 12:31:

> 31 **Wherefore I say unto you, All manner of sin and blasphemy shall be forgiven unto men: but the blasphemy against the Holy Ghost shall not be forgiven unto men.**

We are told that Stephen was filled with the Holy Spirit. These rulers blasphemed against the Holy Spirit when they killed him. There was a lot going on here. In the text, we find Stephen looking up to heaven and saying, "I see the heavens opened, and the Son of man standing on the right hand of God" (Acts 7:56). There was a reason He was standing and not seated. He was preparing to return at their repentance at Stephen's speech. They chose not to repent, but to kill God's messenger.

70

At this stoning, things changed. We are introduced to someone who has never before been mentioned in the Bible. His name is Saul who would later become the Apostle Paul. Acts 7:57-58:

> 57 **Then they cried out with a loud voice, and stopped their ears, and ran upon him [Stephen] with one accord,**

> 58 **And cast him out of the city, and stoned him: and <u>the witnesses laid down their clothes at a young man's feet, whose name was Saul</u>.**

Saul was not a nice guy. To please the rulers, he persecuted the new believers. Acts 8:3:

> 3 **As for Saul, he made havock of the church, entering into every house, and haling men and women committed them to prison.**

Saul received authority from the rulers to go after the new believers following the promise of the kingdom. However, on his way to Damascus, he is confronted by the Risen Savior. Acts 9:3-6:

> 3 **And as he [Saul] journeyed, he came near Damascus: and suddenly there**

shined round about him a light from heaven: 4 **And he fell to the earth, and heard a voice saying unto him, Saul, Saul, why persecutest thou me?**

5 **And he said, Who art thou, Lord? And the Lord said, I am Jesus whom thou persecutest: it is hard for thee to kick against the pricks.**

6 **And he trembling and astonished said, Lord, what wilt thou have me to do? And the Lord said unto him, Arise, and go into the city, and it shall be told thee what thou must do.**

Later, as Paul, he referred to himself as "the chief of sinners" because he had persecuted these believers.

He eventually reached Antioch where a man named Ananias, chosen by God, laid hands upon him to receive his sight. Understandably, Ananias was afraid. Everyone knew Saul and the hatred he had for believers. Notice God's reply to Ananias' hesitation. Acts 9:15-16:

15 **But the Lord said unto him, [Ananias] Go thy way: for <u>he is a chosen vessel unto me</u>, <u>to bear my name before the</u>**

<u>Gentiles, and kings, and the children of Israel:</u>

16 For I will shew him how great things he must suffer for my name's sake.

Since God's calling of Abraham, He only dealt with Israel. You are seeing a dispensational change occurring right here. At this, the remaining seven years of the 490 years were temporarily suspended.

Let's go to the last chapter of the book of Acts to confirm this. God sends the Apostle Paul to "the Gentiles, and kings, and the children of Israel" (v. 15). Paul is addressing the local synagogue in Rome where he was imprisoned. He begins with a quote from the prophet Isaiah. Acts 28:26-27:

26 Saying, Go unto this people, and say, Hearing ye shall hear, and shall not understand; and seeing ye shall see, and not perceive:

27 For the heart of this people is waxed gross, and their ears are dull of hearing, and their eyes have they closed; lest they should see with their eyes, and hear with their ears, and understand with their heart, and should be con-

verted, and I should heal them.

Speaking on God's behalf, he made a proclamation in verse 28:

28 Be it known therefore unto you, that the salvation of God is sent unto the Gentiles, and that they will hear it.

This is the beginning of a new dispensation and its purpose is to offer salvation to the Gentiles "for they will hear it."

It is important to understand that the previous dispensation has not ended. It has been temporarily suspended. The seven remaining years of Daniel's prophecy will be completed. The eternal kingdom promised to David will be established. For this reason, the next dispensation is referred to as a "parenthetical interruption." The Age of Law is temporarily interrupted until this temporary suspension is completed. Then, the remaining seven weeks will resume. What does a temporary suspension look like? It looks like this:

AGE OF LAW	**(AGE OF GRACE)**	**AGE OF LAW**

A parenthetical comment (like hello there) may be included in a sentence, but it does not alter its meaning. For that reason, this present age is referred to as a "parenthetical interruption." The Law of Moses is still in effect. The prophecies and promises God made to Israel will happen, but they are currently held in abeyance until the timeline is restarted.

Most churches and seminaries that teach dispensational theology teach that the Age of Grace follows the Age of Law sequentially – like chapters in a book. They say the Age of Law ends when the Age of Grace begins. This is not correct. What about the remaining seven years to the fulfillment of Daniel's prophecy? Their error has caused confusion for many Christians and makes understanding the end times impossible! Stay with me. I promise that all will become clear as we continue to follow Paul's instructions to Timothy!

Here is the truth. Once the Age of Grace is completed, then the last seven years of the Age of Law will resume. There are two distinct gospels for each of these two ages. We discover this from a meeting between the Twelve Apostles and the Apostle Paul. Galatians 2:1-2:

> **1 Then fourteen years after I [Paul] went up again to Jerusalem with Barnabas,**

and took Titus with me also. 2 And I went up by revelation, and communicated unto them that gospel which I preach among the Gentiles, but privately to them which were of reputation, lest by any means I should run, or had run, in vain.

To be sure that the other apostles, the Twelve, understood the gospel message Paul preached to the Gentiles, he traveled to Jerusalem to meet with them. Galatians 2:7-8:

7 But contrariwise, when they saw that the gospel of the uncircumcision was committed unto me, as the gospel of the circumcision was unto Peter;

8 (For he that wrought effectually in Peter to the apostleship of the circumcision, the same was mighty in me toward the Gentiles:)

A mutual understanding was achieved and an agreement was made among them. Verse 9:

9 And when James, Cephas [Peter], and John, who seemed to be pillars, perceived the grace that was given unto me

[Paul], they gave to me and Barnabas the right hands of fellowship; <u>that we should go unto the heathen, and they unto the circumcision</u>.

Here, the words "heathen" and "uncircumcision" both mean the Gentiles while "circumcision" means the Jews – the children of Abraham. This meeting resulted in an agreement. Paul and Barnabas will take their gospel to the Gentiles while the Twelve will take their gospel to the Jews. That is what it says. You may need to read verses 7 and 9 again to see it.

Anything that is contrary to Scripture is not true. It is a lie. Satan, the father of lies, will do anything to prevent you from understanding the truth. It takes courage and commitment to remain faithful to the Word of God. You are not alone. Jesus Christ is the Living Word. Talk to Him. Ask Him questions as you read this. Trust me. It is worth it. I only present the information. The Holy Spirit does the real teaching! 1 Corinthians 2:13-14:

> 13 **Which things also we speak, not in the words which man's wisdom teacheth, but which the Holy Ghost teacheth; comparing spiritual things with spiritual.**

14 But <u>the natural man receiveth not the things of the Spirit of God</u>: for they are foolishness unto him: neither can he know them, <u>because they are spiritually discerned</u>.

10

No Longer A Mystery

I am sure you have questions. Here are two. "When did the Age of Grace begin?" "When does the Age of Grace end?" Here is another really important one. "If there are two separate gospels, then what's the difference between them?" You need answers to these questions and we get them. Before we move on, think about this. We are studying meat; not milk. The majority of churches that teach biblical truth focus on the milk. This material is for the mature Christian who want to grow in their knowledge of God's Word. Believers have the Holy Spirit to guide them. This material is spiritually "discerned." We must rely on Him for our understanding. Men of learning may say that what we are studying is "foolishness." However, it is the wisdom of God! 1 Corinthians 2:14:

> **14 But the natural man receiveth not the things of the Spirit of God: for they are**

foolishness unto him: neither can he know them, because they are spiritually discerned.

Based upon my observations, I believe the greatest obstacle to understanding the Bible is not the Bible. It is organized religion. Consider all the churches that say they "preach from the Bible" every Sunday. Dedicated church-goers regularly attend these services. I am confident that most of them have never heard what you are studying here. It is almost as if it is hidden. Yet, it is in plain sight.

I attended a fundamental independent church. The people love God and faithfully attend three services a week. Their pastor of some sixty years was pounding on the pulpit. He was yelling at these faithful that they needed to get off the milk and get onto the meat. Milk is the basic simple truths while meat is the deeper truths of God intended for mature believers. He repeated this a couple times. As I sat there, I thought to myself, if the pastor is not preaching them meat, then who will teach them meat? I attended there for a year and was never asked to teach or preach.

Friend, this is spiritual meat! If you are afraid, that fear is not from God. It is from someone who doesn't want you to learn the deeper truths of God.

God wants you to understand the Bible. God desires that ". . . all men to be saved, and to come unto the knowledge of the truth" (1 Tim. 2:4). However, spiritual forces do not want you to know this. I present the information to you the best I know how. But, to truly know God's Word, we must all lean on the Holy Spirit for understanding. The same Holy Spirit that inspired the writers of the Word of God is the same Holy Spirit Who illuminates our understanding. All you need to do is ask!

The Age of Grace

Paul will provide us with the answer to our first question: "When did the Age of Grace begin?" 1 Timothy 1:12-14:

> 12 **And I thank Christ Jesus our Lord, who hath enabled me, for that he counted me faithful, putting me into the ministry; 13 Who was before a blasphemer, and a persecutor, and injurious [to the Jewish believers]: but [now] <u>I obtained mercy</u>, because I did it ignorantly in unbelief.**
>
> 14 <u>**And the grace of our Lord was exceeding abundant with faith and love which is in Christ Jesus.**</u>

Paul admits that he was "the worst of the worst" sinner by calling himself the "chief" of sinners. We continue with verse 15:

> 15 **This is a faithful saying, and worthy of all acceptation, that <u>Christ Jesus came into the world to save sinners; of whom I am chief</u>.**

As the chief of sinners against God, He was an enemy of God. Yet, by grace, God saved him. He didn't earn it. God gave him mercy. Therefore, if God saved Paul, the worst of the worst, then He certainly can save any sinner, right? Verse 16:

> 16 **Howbeit for <u>this cause [reason] I obtained mercy</u>, that <u>in me first</u> Jesus Christ might shew forth all longsuffering, <u>for a pattern [example] to them which should hereafter</u> believe on him to life everlasting.**

Wait a minute! Did we just read that God made Paul to be a pattern or an example for others to follow? Here is the answer to the question. Paul was the first person to be saved by grace through faith! So, the "Age of Grace" began with the conversion of Paul. It was not by his own merit. It was by God's grace!

It wasn't earned or deserved. It was a gift from God. So, when did this Age of Grace begin? It began with the conversion of Paul!

God saved Paul for a reason and we find that reason in the book of Acts. Speaking about Paul, God assures Ananias that ". . . he is a chosen vessel unto me, to bear my name before the Gentiles, and kings, and the children of Israel" (Acts 9:15). Paul received his appointment as an apostle directly from the Risen Lord and God the Father. Galatians 1:1:

> 1 **Paul, an apostle, (<u>not of men, neither by man, but by Jesus Christ, and God the Father, who raised him from the dead</u>;)**

We find that Paul's gospel message wasn't received from the other apostles nor, for that matter, from any other man. Galatians 1:11-12:

> 11 **But I certify you, brethren, <u>that the gospel which was preached of [by] me is</u> not after [from] man.**
>
> 12 **For I neither received it of [from] man, neither was I taught it, but <u>by the revelation of Jesus Christ</u>.**

Following Paul's conversion, he continued to Antioch where his sight was restored. A lot of people miss this completely. From Antioch, he traveled to Arabia. This is the same place where God met face to face with Moses on Mount Sinai! Galatians 1:15-17:

> 15 **But when it pleased God, who separated me from my mother's womb, and <u>called me by his grace,</u> 16 To reveal his Son in [to] me, that I might preach him among the heathen [Gentiles]; immediately I conferred not with flesh and blood [any men]:**

> 17 **Neither went I up to Jerusalem to them which were apostles before me; but [instead] <u>I went into Arabia,</u> and [then] returned again unto Damascus.**

Paul didn't go to Jerusalem immediately after Arabia. He returned to Antioch where he remained separated from the other apostles.

Paul's first meeting with the Twelve came three years later. Verse 18:

> 18 **Then <u>after three years</u> I went up to Jerusalem to see Peter, and abode with him fifteen days.**

Many people, including myself, believe that Paul spent three years in Arabia being taught by the Risen Lord face to face. This would be the same length of time Jesus spent with His Twelve on earth. Since it is not stated, I will leave it to you to decide.

Prior to Paul receiving his gospel message, it had been a complete mystery! The gospel message he received was different from the Twelve. It was never mentioned in Scripture. Paul refers to it as "my gospel." Romans 16:25:

> 25 **Now to him that is of power to stablish you <u>according to my gospel</u>, and the preaching of Jesus Christ, <u>according to the revelation of the mystery, which was kept secret since the world began</u>,**

(See also Rom. 2:16; 2 Tim. 2:8.) We know that it was unknown because the spiritual realm observes everything! This includes the powers, principalities, and rulers of darkness who crucified the Lord. Paul wrote that, if they had known about the Gospel of Grace, then they never would have killed "the Lord of glory." 1 Corinthians 2:7-8:

> 7 **But we speak the wisdom of God in <u>a mystery, even the hidden wisdom, which God ordained before the world</u>**

unto [for] our glory: 8 Which none of the princes of this world knew: for had they known it, they would not have crucified the Lord of glory.

By crucifying the Lord of Glory, these powers, principalities, and rulers of darkness sealed their own doom! Christ was victorious over death.

What is the gospel message entrust to Paul by God. Notice it says "the" gospel by which y'all are saved. This is the most concise statement of the Gospel of Grace. 1 Corinthians 15:1-4:

1 Moreover, brethren, I declare unto you the gospel which I preached unto you, which also ye have received, and wherein ye stand; 2 By which also ye are saved, if ye keep in memory what I preached unto you, unless ye have believed in vain.

3 For I delivered unto you first of all that which I also received, how that [1] Christ died for our sins according to the scriptures; 4 And that [2] he was buried, and that [3] he rose again the third day according to the scriptures:

Again, notice that Paul said this is "the" not "a" gospel message by which they are saved! This is the Gospel of Grace given to the Apostle Paul.

Do you remember how Abraham "believed God" and it was counted to him as righteousness? Today, those who "believe God" and His simple offer of salvation by grace (gift) through faith (believing) will receive God's righteousness! It is not their righteousness that saves them. It is the righteousness of Christ that saves them! Romans 4:21-25:

> 21 **And [Abraham] being fully persuaded that, what he [God] had promised, he [God] was able also to perform.** 22 **And therefore it was imputed [applied] to him [Abraham] for righteousness.**
>
> 23 **Now it was not written for his [Abraham's] sake alone, that it was imputed to him;** 24 **But for us also, to whom it [righteousness] shall be imputed [applied], if we believe on him that raised up Jesus our Lord from the dead;** 25 <u>**Who was delivered for our offences [sins], and was raised again for our justification.**</u>

Those last few works are critical. "For our justification" means that "we are declared by God to be righteous." This is exactly what God did with Abraham. By believing God's promise of salvation in His Word, sinners receive the righteousness. Again, it is not our righteousness, but the righteousness of Christ!

Regardless of who we are or what we have done, those who believe are declared righteous. How? It is because Christ paid the price of salvation in full. Romans 3:22:

> 22 Even **the righteousness of God which is by faith of Jesus Christ unto all and upon all them that believe**: for there is no difference:

This is indeed wonderful news. If you have ever doubted your salvation, then put your mind at ease. Our salvation has been purchased for us by the blood of God's dear Son. Everyone who believes the Gospel of Grace preached by Paul will be saved. Salvation is not based upon merit at all and, thus, there is no difference!

11

A Heavenly Inheritance

We still have a few more questions to answer. The next one we'll jump on is, "What is the difference between the Gospel of Grace and the Gospel of the Kingdom?" Here is another statement about the Gospel of Grace. Ephesians 2:8-9:

> 8 **For by grace are ye saved through faith; and that not of yourselves: it is the gift of God:** 9 **Not of works, lest any man should boast.**

The word "grace" means "gift" and the word "faith" means "believing what God said." We receive salvation as a gift by believing God. Paul continues by saying that it is not by our own "works." This means that we don't have to "do" anything to earn it. Remember this: Christ did it all!

Paul established groups of grace believers. Those who taught the Mosaic Law would try to add other requirements for salvation. In the Gospel of Grace, works play no part in receiving salvation. Paul warned the assembly in Galatia about this. Anything added to what Christ has already finished changes it into another gospel. Galatians 1:6-7:

> 6 **I marvel that ye are so soon removed from him that called you into the grace of Christ <u>unto another gospel</u>:**
>
> 7 **<u>Which is not another;</u> but there be some that trouble you, and would <u>pervert the gospel of Christ</u>.**

By adding works to the Gospel of Grace, they made it into another gospel which is not good news at all. There are still churches today that add requirements to the Gospel of Grace. Do not fall for this false gospel. It is not a gospel. It is not "good news" at all.

Here is the biggest problem for some people. The Gospel of Grace is too simple. If it is really that simple, then a lot of religions would go out of business. Again, the biggest threat to the Gospel of Grace is organized religion. Most churches are driven by two things: the size of the attendance and the size of offerings. Many of them dispense salvation based upon their own devised customs and traditions. They determine the worthiness of the church-goer. Paul warns believers about this. Colossians 2:8:

> 8 **Beware lest any man spoil you through philosophy [of men] and vain deceit, after the tradition of men, after the rudiments of the world, and not after Christ.**

Salvation is free. It is a gift of God paid for by His Son. It is available to anyone through faith. Faith is not doing. Faith is believing the Word of God!

So, why isn't the Gospel of Grace preached in more churches today? The answer is simple: foolishness! (See 1 Cor. 1:18, 21, 23, 25; 2:14; 3:19.) Most people are taught and encouraged to earn their salvation. They must achieve a higher level of righteousness than others beside them. However, salvation is not based upon a merit basis! That is the wisdom of men. That is human pride. But, for those who will humble themselves and admit they are sinners in need of a Savior, God offers the only solution—for free!

Friend, as we continue, you will find there is so much more to this than salvation. The book of Ephesians was written to let believers know who they are "in Christ." Salvation is a gift given to those who believe without any requirement of works. Like I just said, there is so much more! In the following, Paul wrote to those saved by grace though faith. Ephesians 1:12-13:

> 12 **That we [those who believed] should be to the praise of his glory, who first trusted in Christ.**
>
> 13 **In whom ye also trusted, after that ye heard the word of truth, the gospel of your salvation: in whom also after that ye believed, <u>ye were sealed with that holy Spirit of promise,</u>**

When someone believes, they immediately receive the "holy Spirit of Promise." The Holy Spirit resides in us permanently. There is a promise of an inheritance that comes with the Holy Spirit! Verse 14:

> 14 **Which [Who] is <u>the earnest of our inheritance</u> until the redemption of the purchased possession, unto the praise of his glory.**

The word "earnest" has a special meaning here. It is still used in the real estate transactions today. It means "the deposit which guarantees the completion of the promised transaction." What is this transaction that the Holy Spirit guarantees?

Paul explains that only half of our redemption has been completed. Spiritually, we were placed in Christ Who is seated at the right hand of God. This happened upon our salvation. Presently, we remain in our earthly bodies as we wait for the other half of our redemption. That will complete the transaction of our redemption. Ephesians 2:4-6:

> 4 **But God, who is rich in mercy, for his great love wherewith he loved us,** 5 **Even when we were dead in sins, <u>hath quickened us [made us alive] together with Christ</u>, (by grace ye are saved;)**
>
> 6 **And hath raised us up together, and <u>made us sit together in heavenly places in Christ Jesus</u>:**

Spiritually, believers are presently "in Christ" while our bodies remain here on earth. The holy Spirit of Promise guarantees the completion of our redemption. When will this "bodily redemption" happen? There is a "calling away" of those saved by grace through faith. The words "His Calling" in the Bible refer to the "Rapture."

When we see the words "His Calling" it refers to this future event. Later, we will see that Christ appears in the sky and "calls" His believers to Himself. It is the promise of "His Calling" that gives every believer wonderful hope! Ephesians 1:18:

18 The eyes of your understanding being enlightened; that ye may know what is <u>the hope of his calling</u>, and what [are] <u>the riches of the glory of his inheritance in the saints,</u>

Ephesians is truly a wonderful book. It teaches believers who they are "in Christ" and encourages them with the hope of His Calling. There is so much more for believers. Our redemption and salvation are safe and secure in Christ. We have the riches of His inheritance because we are "in Christ."

Now, let's look at this inheritance. The very first verse in the Bible gives us an important clue. God divided His Creation in the heaven and the earth. Genesis 1:1:

1 In the beginning God created <u>the heaven</u> and <u>the earth.</u>

Grace Believers will receive a heavenly inheritance when they are called to Him. Those saved by the

Gospel of the Kingdom will receive a different inheritance. The eternal Kingdom of David will be on the earth. Israel, saved by the Kingdom Gospel, will serve the eternal King as He reigns over His earthly Kingdom from Jerusalem.

As we have seen, the Age of Law is in temporary suspension until the end of the Age of Grace. Now, we can answer the question: "When does the Age of Grace end? Paul, in his explanation to the Gentiles, gives the answer. Romans 11:25-27:

> 25 **For I would not, brethren, that ye should be ignorant of this mystery, lest ye should be wise in your own conceits;** <u>**that blindness in part is happened to Israel, until the fulness of the Gentiles be come in.**</u>
>
> 26 **And so all Israel shall be saved: as it is written, There shall come out of Sion the Deliverer, and shall turn away ungodliness from Jacob:** 27 <u>**For this is my covenant unto them, when I shall take away their sins.**</u>

The completion of the Age of Grace is based upon this. Once "the fulness of the Gentiles be come in," then the Rapture will occur. Jesus will appear in the heavens and call His own to meet Him in the air. 1 Thessalonians 4:15-17:

> 15 **For this we say unto you by the word of the Lord, that we which are alive and remain unto the coming of the Lord shall not prevent [precede] them which are asleep.**

> 16 **For the Lord himself shall descend from heaven with a shout, with the voice of the archangel, and with the trump of God: and the dead in Christ shall rise first:**

> 17 **Then we which are alive and remain <u>shall be caught up together with them in the clouds, to meet the Lord in the air:</u> and <u>so shall we ever be with the Lord</u>.**

The Grace Believers' inheritance is heavenly and they will be with the Lord forever. Daniel's timeline still has seven years to run. Those who remain must endure the Tribulation. It begins with the appearance of the Antichrist and the people of this prince. In spite of everything, all that God promised in Daniel's prophecy will be fulfilled!

12

An Earthly Inheritance

The Age of Grace began with the conversion of the Apostle Paul and ended with the Rapture. Once the Age of Grace has ended, Daniel's timeline will resume. In His earthly ministry, Jesus referred to the Kingdom as being "at hand" implying, at that time, it was imminent. (See Matt. 3:2, 4:17, 10:7; Mk. 1:15, 15:43; Lk. 21:31.) Until it was suspended, the seven years would have continued to the Kingdom. The Jews called Jesus "the Son of David" because they were familiar with the promise to King David. In this chapter, we will look at Israel's earthly inheritance.

God separated Israel from the Gentiles for a reason to be revealed at the end. They are to become a nation of priests. (See Ex. 19:6.) Israel will be intricately involved in God's restoration of Creation! For Israel, everything in their future centers on Daniel's timeline. The angel Gabriel gave him a timeline that went far beyond the restoration of Jerusalem. It was for the complete restoration of Creation, but also the establishment of the eternal Kingdom! Look at the six items to be accomplished in Daniel 9:24:

> 24 **Seventy weeks are determined upon thy people and upon thy holy city, to [1] finish the transgression, and [2] to make an end of sins, and [3] to make reconciliation for iniquity, and [4] to bring in everlasting righteousness, and [5] to seal up the vision and prophecy, and [6] to anoint the most Holy.**

The "most Holy" is the Messiah, the Son of God. The seventy weeks are actually seventy weeks of years totaling four hundred ninety years. At the end, the Kingdom will be established and the Most Holy One anointed King.

Daniel's prophecy assured the Jews that their promises will come true as well as what will happen along the way. This material is important enough for us to repeat it. For "repetition is the mother of all learning." Verses 25-26:

> 25 **Know therefore and understand, that from the going forth of the commandment to restore and to build Jerusalem unto the Messiah the Prince shall be**

seven weeks, and threescore and two weeks: the street shall be built again, and the wall, even in troublous times.

26 And after [the] threescore and two weeks [1] shall Messiah be cut off, but not for himself: and [2] the people of the prince [Antichrist] that shall come shall destroy the city [Jerusalem] and the sanctuary [temple]; and the end thereof shall be with a flood, and unto the end of the war desolations are determined.

These verses are the key to understanding Israel's future. The crucifixion marked the end of the sixty-nineth week or 483 years of the total 490.

Of the seventy weeks, there remains only one week. After the Rapture, the suspension will be lifted and this is how it will unfold. It begins with the appearance of the Antichrist in verse 27:

27 And he [Antichrist] shall confirm the covenant with many <u>for one week</u>: and in the midst of the week he shall cause the sacrifice and the oblation to cease, and for the overspreading of abominations he shall make it desolate, even until the consummation, and that deter-

mined shall be poured upon the desolate.

Some people confuse the Rapture or His Appearing with His Second Coming. Here is the difference. At the Rapture, Jesus Christ will appear in the air and call those saved by the Gospel of Grace to Himself. They are called "the Body of Christ" for good reason. However, the Second Coming will occur at the end of the Tribulation. Then, Jesus Christ will physically return to earth for one purpose. He will save Israel and destroy their enemies.

Like the refiner's fire, these seven years are called Jacob's time of trouble. All Israel's faith will be tested. Jeremiah 30:7

> 7 **Alas! for <u>that day is great, so that none is like it</u>: it is even <u>the time of Jacob's trouble</u>; but he shall be saved out of it.**

Israel's history includes their accomplishments as well as their failures. God held them to the Mosaic Covenant. When they obeyed God and followed His Law, He blessed them. When they failed, God punished them. Israel's greatest failure was lack of faith. They did not believe God's Word, but chose to reject it and go their own way.

During the Pentecost Feast, the Apostle Peter addressed the Jews attending the festival. Being filled with the Spirit, the new Kingdom Believers spilled out onto the street appearing to be drunk. Notice Peter's response. Acts 2:15-16:

> 15 **For these are not drunken, as ye suppose, seeing it is but the third hour of the day.** 16 **But <u>this is that which was spoken by the prophet Joel</u>;**

The Jews cannot claim that they were not told. Peter continued with the prophecy. Verses 17-20:

> 17 **And it shall come to pass in the last days, saith God, I will pour out of my Spirit upon all flesh: and your sons and your daughters shall prophesy, and your young men shall see visions, and your old men shall dream dreams:** 18 **And on my servants and on my handmaidens I will pour out in those days of my Spirit; and they shall prophesy:**
>
> 19 **And I will shew wonders in heaven above, and signs in the earth beneath; blood, and fire, and vapour of smoke:** 20 **The sun shall be turned into darkness,**

and the moon into blood, before that great and notable day of the Lord come:

All this will happen during the final seven years. There is hope for Israel but only those who have faith. Verse 21:

21 And it shall come to pass, that whosoever shall call on the name of the Lord shall be saved.

Peter included a proclamation to the children of Israel making an indictment or charge against them. Verses 22-23:

22 <u>Ye men of Israel, hear these words</u>; Jesus of Nazareth, a man approved of God among you by miracles and wonders and signs, which God did by him in the midst of you, as ye yourselves also know:

23 Him, being delivered by the determinate counsel and foreknowledge of God, <u>ye have taken, and by wicked hands have crucified and slain</u>:

Peter would write later in a letter to Jewish believers about Israel's inheritance. 1 Peter 1:3-5:

3 Blessed be the God and Father of our Lord Jesus Christ, which according to his abundant mercy hath begotten us again unto a lively hope by the resurrection of Jesus Christ from the dead,

4 <u>To an inheritance</u> incorruptible, and undefiled, and that fadeth not away, <u>reserved in heaven for you</u>, **5** Who are <u>kept by the power of God</u> through faith unto salvation <u>ready to be revealed in the last time</u>.

Their inheritance has been prepared for them. It is held for them until the point in time when God chooses to reveal it. Israel's inheritance is earthly, but kept safely for them in heaven. You might ask, "So, what is it?"

To find the answer we will go to the book of Revelation where the conclusion of God's restoration is recorded. Daniel's original prayer asked God about the restoration of Jerusalem. This is a special city and has always been dear to the hearts of the children of Israel. Let us look at the verses to hear how God will reveal their inheritance. The Apostle John first mentions the "New Jerusalem" in Revelation 3:12:

12 Him that overcometh will I make a pillar in the temple of my God, and he shall go no more out: and I will write upon him the name of my God, and <u>the name of the city of my God, which is new Jerusalem, which cometh down out of heaven from my God</u>: and I will write upon him my new name.

The focal point here is that their inheritance is earthly based. We are told that it "cometh down out of heaven from my God."

John compares the New Jerusalem to the radiance of a bride in Revelation 21:2-3:

2 And I John saw <u>the holy city, new Jerusalem, coming down from God out of heaven</u>, prepared as a bride adorned for her husband.

3 And I heard a great voice out of heaven saying, Behold, the tabernacle of God is with men, and he will dwell with them, and they shall be his people, and God himself shall be with them, and be their God.

Not only will their inheritance be to receive the New Jerusalem, but God will "tabernacle" or "dwell" with them on earth. He will be Emanu-El which, in Hebrew, means "God with us."

We have looked at two different inheritances. This would confirm that there must be two separate and distinct heirs. The inheritances stem from the two different gospel messages given to each, but only Israel received prophecies concerning their future. Why? The Gospel of Grace remained a secret from before the foundations of the earth until revealed to the Apostle Paul. This group was removed at the Rapture. Now, the spotlight is on Israel and their prophetic future. Between Daniel's timeline and John's book of Revelation, God has confirmed that what He has said, He will accomplish.

In the next chapter, we will make a comparison between these two gospel messages placing them side-by-side.

13

Side-By-Side

People make the simplest things so difficult. With everyone teaching the Bible "their way," it is hard to decide who you can trust. Remember this. We can always trust God's Word. The key to understanding the Bible is understanding how God laid it out. Once you do, you can read it for yourself. Christians attend church most of their lives and have never heard some of this material. Someone told me that once people understand that salvation is a gift and it's free, they won't need the clergy anymore. Talk about loss of job security. That may be possible, but I think pastors and teachers only know what they themselves have been taught. Then, they too teach what they were taught. To those of you who have come this far in the book, I say bravo!

No one wants to be told they are wrong. No one wants to change what they believe. Even if the Lord Jesus Christ came and spoke to them in person, the religious establishment wouldn't listen. It challenged their customs and traditions. Today, they hold in their hands the written Word of God. I have watched them wave the Bible over their heads, but preach their own philosophies. And, when they are confronted with the truth, well, you will not be attending that church anymore. So, congratulations! You allowed me to present to you the entire Bible systematically. The dispensational system is a tool. You can apply it yourself as you read the Bible. We used biblical text to support this summary. When you finish this book, you can test it yourself.

So far, we know there are two gospels. One gospel is for the Jews, the "circumcision." The other gospel is for the Gentiles, the "uncircumcision." Remember the conclusion of the meeting in Jerusalem. All of the apostles including Paul met together. Galatians 2:7-8:

> 7 **But contrariwise, when they saw that the gospel of the uncircumcision was committed unto me [Paul], as the gospel of the circumcision was unto Peter; 8 (For he that wrought effectually in Peter to the apostleship of the circumcision, the same was mighty in me toward the Gentiles:)**

There being two gospel messages, they must be different. Let's compare them by putting them side by side.

The Gospel of the Kingdom

The majority of churches present the Bible as one book. They teach there is only one theme—Jesus Christ Who died on the Cross. That is true and doesn't change. However, God applies this singular event differently: one way for the Jews and another way for the Gentiles. Unfortunately, most Bible teachers blend these two gospels into one! No wonder people are confused because their teachers are. However, like a good tradesperson, you have studied. You learned there are divisions in the Bible. Now, when you read God's Word, rightly divided, we will not be ashamed or embarrassed as Paul instructed Timothy on this subject. 2 Timothy 2:15:

> 15 **Study to shew thyself approved unto God, <u>a workman that needeth not to be ashamed, rightly dividing the word of truth</u>.**

You now have this valuable tool! As you go on, remember this. Truth is never popular. Hold truth in your heart and do not be deterred.

Most Christians are taught that the "Church" began at Pentecost. Do you remember Jesus speaking about the fields being ripe for harvest? This was the result of Jesus and the Twelve planting the seed of the gospel. Wait, what gospel are we talking about? It is the "gospel to the circumcision" committed to Peter and the others by Jesus Christ Himself. It is the Gospel of the Kingdom! (See Gal. 2:7-9.)

In Matthew 10:2-4, Jesus named each of the twelve disciples individually. Then, in the verses that follow, He gave specific instructions to them. Matthew 10:5-7:

> 5 **These twelve Jesus sent forth, and commanded them, saying, <u>Go not into the way of the Gentiles</u>, and into any city of the Samaritans enter ye not: 6 <u>But go rather to the lost sheep of the house of Israel</u>. 7 And as ye go, <u>preach, saying, The kingdom of heaven is at hand</u>.**

The kingdom was promised to David and to his Heir Who is Christ the King. With the kingdom being "at hand," this message was sent to the Jews alone.

The Jewish festival of Pentecost happens fifty days after Passover. It has another name which is the Festival of First Fruits. In other words, it celebrates the first portion of the harvest. These new Kingdom Believers were the "first fruits" of the "kingdom harvest." Jesus and the Twelve had planted seeds for this harvest during His ministry to "the lost sheep of the house of Israel." Looking back, we see this from Luke 10:1-2:

> 1 After these things <u>the Lord appointed other seventy</u> also, and sent them two and two before his face into every city and place, whither he himself would come.

> 2 Therefore said he unto them, <u>The harvest truly is great, but the labourers are few: pray ye therefore the Lord of the harvest, that he would send forth labourers into his harvest</u>.

If this was not the beginning of the "Church," let's consider what happened at Pentecost – the Festival of First Fruits. The following was recorded by Luke in Acts 2. These Kingdom Believers were told to wait in the Upper Room for the gift of the Comforter. In the street below, the noisy crowd swarmed. These Jews came from many countries to celebrate this Jewish festival. Peter gave a speech to these Jews who questioned what was happening. He refuted that these new believers were drunk, but were instead the fulfillment of a prophecy from the Hebrew prophet Joel. Acts 2:14-18:

> 14 But Peter, standing up with the eleven, lifted up his voice, and said unto them, Ye men of Judaea, and all ye that dwell at Jerusalem, be this known unto you, and hearken to my words: 15 For these are not drunken, as ye suppose, seeing it is but the third hour of the day. 16 But this is that which was spoken by the prophet Joel;
>
> 17 And it shall come to pass in the last days, saith God, I will pour out of my Spirit upon all flesh: and your sons and your daughters shall prophesy, and your young men shall see visions, and your old men shall dream dreams: 18 And on my servants and on my handmaidens I will pour out in those days of my Spirit; and they shall prophesy:

Peter lists some natural signs that confirm that he is speaking about the end times. Verses 19-20:

> 19 And I will shew wonders in heaven above, and signs in the earth beneath; blood, and fire, and vapour of smoke:

20 The sun shall be turned into darkness, and the moon into blood, before that great and notable day of the Lord come:

These are described events are part of the Tribulation. The Coming of the Christ is referred to as "that great and notable day of the Lord."

Peter's speech is a summary of their long history of all that the Jews have done against Him. The Old Testament is filled with their rejection and lack of faith. From its content, it is clear that Peter is talking to the Jews. He concludes with this proclamation. Acts 2:36:

36 Therefore let all the house of Israel know assuredly, that God hath made that same Jesus, whom ye have crucified, both Lord and Christ.

These accusations can only be applied to the Jews. They murdered their prophets and, in the end, they killed their Messiah and King! Now, notice their response in verse 37:

37 Now when they heard this, they were pricked in their heart, and said unto

Peter and to the rest of the apostles, **Men and brethren, what shall we do?**

They were cut to the quick. They were convicted and ask their brethren, "What shall we do?" Here, we must pay close attention to Peter's response. He tells them how to be saved according to the Gospel of the Kingdom. Verse 38:

> 38 Then Peter said unto them, **Repent, and be baptized** every one of you in the name of Jesus Christ **for the remission of sins**, and ye shall receive the gift of the Holy Ghost.

If they follow Peter's instructions, then they will receive "the remission of sins." Anyone who is familiar with cancer knows that "remission" does not mean a "cure." Here, the word "remission" does not mean "forgiveness," but rather the putting aside of their sins until the Messiah returns. It will be at that time that the sins of faithful Jews will be forgiven. Let's make sure there is no confusion. Peter states exactly who this promise applies to. Verse 39:

> 39 For the promise is unto you, and to your children, and to all that are afar off, even as many as the Lord our God shall call.

Hold on a minute. Their sins are forgiven when? The entire chapter of Matthew 24 concerns these last seven years. In it, Jesus answered questions from His disciples about the end times. This verse will confirm when the sins of faithful Jews will be forgiven. Matthew 24:13:

> 13 But he <u>that shall endure unto the end</u>, the same shall be saved.

The Gospel of the Kingdom also requires Jews to continually prove their faith by their actions. Simply put, Israel's history of losing faith warranted this. Like Abraham, their actions will prove their faith. Look at what the Apostle James wrote in his letter sent "to the twelve tribes which are scattered abroad" (Jas. 1:1). He used Abraham as his example. James 2:18-24:

> 18 Yea, a man may say, Thou hast faith, and I have works: shew me thy faith without thy works, and I will shew thee my faith by my works. 19 Thou believest that there is one God; thou doest well: the devils also believe, and tremble.

> 20 But wilt thou know, O vain man, that faith without works is dead? 21 <u>Was not Abraham our father justified by works</u>,

when he had offered Isaac his son upon the altar? 22 <u>Seest thou how faith wrought [worked] with his works, and by works was faith made perfect?</u>

23 And the scripture was fulfilled which saith, <u>Abraham believed God, and it was imputed unto him for righteousness</u>: and he was called the Friend of God. 24 Ye see then how that by works a man is justified, and not by faith only.

When the Grace Believers are removed, God's offer of salvation by grace through faith is also withdrawn. The Age of Law resumes. It will be the Gospel of the Kingdom that will be preached. "Wait, are you sure?" You will recognize these following verses, but we have added one more verse. See Jesus' words concerning the gospel to be preached. Matthew 24:11-14:

11 And many false prophets shall rise, and shall deceive many. 12 And because iniquity shall abound, the love of many shall wax cold.

13 <u>But he that shall endure unto the end, the same shall be saved.</u> 14 And <u>this gospel of the kingdom</u> shall be preached in

all the world for a witness unto all nations; and <u>then shall the end come</u>.

during the seven years of the Tribulation. They must endure to the end to be saved. It is "the Gospel of the Kingdom" that will be preached in all the world. And then, the end shall come.

The Gospel of Grace

Paul gave a warning to anyone who mixes the above requirements with the Gospel of Grace. Preachers merge these two gospels into one all the time while ignoring the apparent conflict. A group called the Judaizers deceived Grace Believers by adding the requirements of the Law to Paul's gospel. Writing to the assembly in Galatia, Paul gave this stern warning. Galatians 1:6-9:

> **6 I marvel that ye are so soon removed from him that called you into the grace of Christ <u>unto another gospel</u>: 7 <u>Which is not another; but there be some that trouble you, and would pervert the gospel of Christ</u>.**
>
> **8 But though we, or an angel from heaven, preach <u>any other gospel unto you than that which we have preached</u>**

unto you, let him be accursed. 9 **As we said before, so say I now again, If any man preach any other gospel unto you than that ye have received, let him be accursed.**

The Galatians received the Gospel of Grace from Paul. This gospel is simple! The Lord Jesus Christ did everything necessary for their salvation. Their sins aren't in remission, but completely forgiven! By adding anything to the Gospel of Grace, it makes it another gospel which is not "good news" at all!

There were no promises, covenants, or prophecies in the Old Testament concerning the Gentiles. The Gospel of Grace was a mystery – hidden in God. It was completely unknown even to the angelic hosts. The powers and principalities of darkness were completely unaware "for had they known it, they would not have crucified the Lord of glory" (1 Cor. 2:8).

Compare this to the Gospel of Grace where Christ did it all. Salvation is immediately received by faith alone. There are no miracles, signs, or wonders. Faith is believing what Jesus Christ did through His death, burial, and resurrection. Salvation is by grace through faith alone. Believing what Christ did for us is sufficient for our salvation. We were bought by His blood. We are a purchased possession and eternally secure in Him. This makes sense when we see what Paul wrote in Galatians 5:1:

> 1 **Stand fast therefore in the liberty wherewith Christ hath made us free, and be not entangled again with the yoke of bondage.**

We were once slaves to sin. Now we've been bought back – redeemed by the blood of our Savior. All this was accomplished for us because of Who Christ is and what He has done. Our salvation is by God's grace We received it through faith alone. Our inheritance is secure "in Christ!"

14

Final Words

The purpose of this book was to provide you with the basic structure or framework of the entire Bible. It is my favorite book with so much to discover! Hopefully, you have learned about a new tool, seen how it is used, and will continue to test it yourself. You can go deeper into studying the Bible and learn additional tools. Consider other resources available through GraceWord Publishing.

You may not have seen the Bible rightly divided into Age or dispensations. Now you can see it in a different light. No Scripture was removed or altered while presenting the material. My own notes, shown in brackets within the verses, were intended to clarify the meaning for you. Later, the quoted verses can be read without the bracketed comments and within its context in any King James Bible.

As promised, we built an imaginary framework or bookcase. You can use it to store and organize your knowledge about the Bible. Divided into dispensations or ages you can index your thoughts. You now know that the entire Bible was written "**for**" you, but not all the Bible was written "**to**" you. Reading the Bible from cover to cover like it was a copy of *War and Peace,* a very large novel, ends with frustration. If you are a Gentile, then I suggest you start with the portion of the Bible written "**to**" you. Let me give you another tool or "key" to use. It may sound silly, but my "jumbo paperclip method" works!

As silly as this sounds crazy, but go ahead and try it. Be a big kid and listen to your teacher. You will need a "jumbo paperclip." Find the book of Romans which is Paul's first letter. It comes right after the book of Acts. Then, find his last letter of Philemon. It comes just before Hebrews. Now, hold all of Paul's books together and slide the paperclip over them to hold them together. If you don't want to use a jumbo paperclip, then you can use two bookmarks. You have separated Paul's letters from the rest of the books. Once you realize how little you have to read to understand how the Bible applies to you, as a Gentile, you will be pleasantly surprised.

This exercise is designed to make a visual impression in your mind. Most people miss this completely. They read the Bible like it is one big book. However, Paul's thirteen letters were written specifically to Gentiles. So, if you're a Gentile, then these letters were written *to* you! If you are a Jew, the books in the New Testament that come before and those that come after Paul's letters were written "to" you. Of course, anyone can read any of the books. It is just important to remember who they were written to.

We are presently in the Age of Grace. There is an offer currently on the table. You know that in order for an offer to be binding or effective, the offer must be accepted. However, in order for someone to accept the offer, they must first know what the offer is, right? The title of this book is *The Hidden Gospel*. The subtitle refers to this offer. This good news was *Once A Mystery But Now Revealed*. In this book, I want to make that offer very clear to you. I want it clear enough for you to either accept or reject it. Remember, the choice is yours to make.

But now, you should know that the Age of Grace has a gospel message different from the Jews. You should know that the covenants and promises God made to Israel were not intended for the

Gentiles. Most churches teach these covenants and promises were transferred to the "Church." This is called "replacement theology" and it is a lie. You have seen what the Word of God says. The Gospel of Grace was a mystery and it was hidden until the Risen Lord revealed it to Paul. As God told Ananias, " . . . Go thy way: for he is a chosen vessel unto me, to bear my name before the Gentiles, and kings, and the children of Israel" (Acts 9:15). He is the Apostle appointed by God to the Gentiles. Paul said, "For I speak to you Gentiles, inasmuch as I am the apostle of the Gentiles . . . " (Rom. 11:13).

We must not straddle fences. We must not mix different dispensations. It creates "blenderized" theology where we will be ashamed or embarrassed before God. Paul warned Timothy, "Study to shew thyself approved unto God, a workman that needeth not to be ashamed, rightly dividing the word of truth" (2 Tim. 2:15). I have another story for you. I was teaching a Bible class for adults at the local Baptist Church founded in 1827. There were about ten people there. I presented this information to them over the course of several weeks. One woman made a statement, "I've been going to this church since I was born. No one ever explained the Bible this way." She was in her early seventies. She continued, "Finally, the Bible makes sense!" Those are words that delight any Bible teacher. I can only teach and present the information. It is the Holy Spirit Who makes it make sense.

This story continues. We lived in the land of ice and snow. So, many would spend their winters in Florida where she attended a Bible-preaching church. A friend asked her if she still believed what she learned at the Bible study. Her response was disheartening, "I spoke to my pastor here in Florida. He had never heard of such a thing. He told me that it would be best if I stayed away from this." Heard to hear it and believe the truth, but it's easy to lose faith in the truth. Most people just reject it upfront because they have never heard such non-sense. Do you remember my discussion about "foolishness?" In chapters one and four, I mentioned this word over a dozen times and mostly underlined in the verses.

We are all sinners – everyone of us. Each of us is related to Adam who sinned. What is the consequence of sin? Romans 6:23:

> 23 For <u>the wages of sin is death</u>; but <u>the gift of God is eternal life</u> through Jesus Christ our Lord.

Look! The consequence of sin and its solution are found in the same verse. Wow! This verse says a lot. As sinners, we are condemned to death. Then, Paul tells us that the solution is a "gift!" When a gift is received, it there any expectation that it must be paid for or is it free?

Paul admitted that he was a sinner and calls himself the chief sinner because he persecuted the early believers. 1 Timothy 1:15:

> **15 This is a faithful saying, and worthy of all acceptation, that Christ Jesus came into the world to save sinners; of whom I am chief.**

If God can save Paul, the chief sinner, then God can save anyone who believes. With that as the core of the Gospel of Grace, Paul became our "pattern" to follow. He made this clear in verse 16:

> **16 Howbeit for this cause I obtained mercy, <u>that in me first</u> Jesus Christ might shew forth all longsuffering, <u>for a pattern to them which should hereafter believe on him to life everlasting</u>.**

The Jews who follow the Kingdom Gospel follow their Messiah. Those saved by the Gospel of Grace follow Jesus the Son of God by following Paul's example. Salvation is by grace through faith without works. The importance of Paul's example or pattern in this current dispensation can't be overstressed. Think about this for a moment. Here is my point. How important is it for us, in this Age of Grace, to read and understand Paul's teaching?

I have another story. A young boy tugged on Paul's cloak and asked him what he needed to do to be saved. Paul, looking down at the boy, told him there was nothing he could do. The boy's eyes filled with tears. Then, Paul continued. He told him that everything that needed to be done for him to be saved had already been done. He knelt beside the boy. When Jesus died on the Cross, He died in his place and paid the price for all his sins. After He died, they buried Him. But, Jesus was a righteous Man and God raised Him from the dead because He had no sin. He took our punishment for us. The boy smiled. He understood there was nothing he needed to do. Paul asked him if he believed that Jesus did all this for him. Regardless of your age, this story could be about you. Like the young boy, you need to answer this question for yourself.

The finished work of Christ's death, burial, and resurrection is sufficient to meet the requirements of God righteousness. Paul wrote to the Ephesians that once we believe, we receive the righteousness of Christ. So, it is not our righteousness that saves us.

Paul makes it clear that the righteousness we receive is Christ's righteousness. Therefore, all the glory belongs to Him. Ephesians 1:6-9:

> 6 **To the praise of the glory of his grace, wherein he hath made us accepted in the beloved.**
>
> 7 **In whom we have redemption through his blood, the forgiveness of sins, according to the riches of his grace;** 8 **Wherein he hath abounded toward us in all wisdom and prudence;**
>
> 9 **Having made known unto us the mystery of his will, according to his good pleasure which he hath purposed in himself:**

All this is according to the wisdom of God as He works His plan to restore His Creation. The Jews received their offer as a people. It was sent to "the lost sheep of the house of Israel" (Matt. 10:6; 15:24). The offer was made to Abraham's children "to confirm the promises made to the fathers" (Rom. 15:8). Now, in this present Age of Grace, God offers salvation to both Gentiles and Jews individually. It is free to all who will receive it through faith. It is my sincere hope that this book has provided you with a summary and a valuable tool for you to apply to Scripture yourself. As I said before, I can only present the truth as best I can. It is the Holy Spirit Who works to do the will of "God our Saviour." 1 Timothy 2:3-4:

> 3 **For this is good and acceptable in the sight of God our Saviour;**

> 4 <u>**Who will have all men to be saved, and to come unto the knowledge of the truth.**</u>

Where should you go from here? If all of the information presented to you is new, then you will want to test it for yourself. When learning to use a new tool, sometimes it's best way to first watch someone else using it. A student might graduate from a trade school, but their confidence comes from working with someone experienced in that trade as an apprentice. There are thirteen books written by Paul. These are the books included inside the paperclip. An expositional commentary, rightly divided, will take you through a book of the Bible verse-by-verse. Yes, it will be the author's interpretation, but you see how someone experienced applies the tool. You will get to a point where you can choose to agree or disagree with the author. This is fine as long as you can support your conclusion with biblical texts.

If you have accepted God's offer of salvation by grace through faith recently, I suggest you read the commentary on Ephesians first. Why? Paul explains in that book who we, as Grace Believers, are "in Christ." God is giving us so much more than salvation. It is one of my favorite books. On the other hand, if you are looking the definitive book on Pauline theology, then it would be Romans. All of Paul's epistles are great! If you already feel comfortable with my approach to Scripture, then consider reading one of the commentaries published by Grace-Word Publishing.

Respectfully,
Dr. David Alan Greene

Resources

Here are some resources I would recommend. Personally, if you need good news, then you need to start with the commentary on Ephesians. Once you are saved, it answers the question, "Who am I in Christ?" It also goes into the abundance prepared for those who believe by faith.

My dear friends Steve and Stephanie Tackett offer many resources. Steve has taught rightly dividing and the Gospel of Grace for over twenty-five years. He breaks the Bible down and explains it dispensationally. He has written two commentaries. There are live weekly online classes, recorded classes, and audio recordings on Grace Bible Network's website is: www.gracebiblenetwork.org.

The Berean Bible Society has been around for many years. They offer a free monthly publication. All you have to do is sign up online. They have online classes, books, and host regional Bible conferences as well. www.bereanbiblesociety.org.

Rev. Byron Wiggans, a local pastor, teaches his congregation and provides recorded classes. There are also links to various resources on this website: www.gracebelieversbiblestudy.com.

There is a list of churches preaching the Word of God rightly divided called "grace churches." As of this writing, this list is maintained and updated regularly: www.gracechurches.wordpress.com.

Finally, you can check out the list of other publications from GraceWord Publishing. Their website is: www.gracewordpublishing.com. If you have question, I encourage you to use the Contact Us form on the website.

Other GraceWord Publications

In English

1st Corinthians: Dispensationally Considered
1st & 2nd Thessalonians: Dispensationally Con.
1st & 2nd Timothy & Titus: Dispensationally Con.
2nd Corinthians: Dispensationally Considered
Acts: Dispensationally Considered
Colossians & Philemon: Dispensationally Con.
Ephesians: Dispensationally Considered
Galatians: Dispensationally Considered
Hebrews: Dispensationally Considered
How Am I Wired? Change Begins With Und.
Letters To Theophilus – Are You Ready For . . .
Philippians: Dispensationally Considered
Romans: Dispensationally Considered
The Glorious Destiny Of Israel – The Fulfillment . . .
The Hebrew Epistles: Dispensationally Considered
Two Distinct Gospel Messages Of The New Test.

En español

Cartas A Teofilo: ¿Estás listo para los últimos . . .
Efesios: Dispensacionalmente considerado . . .

Letters To Theophilus provides a deeper understanding of three systems used by most evangelical churches to interpret the Bible. These systems are explained. Each is then tested using a test of truth. A successful system must apply to the entire Bible and there can be no failure. The book delves into the Word of Truth using the dispensational tool. It is worth it. The result of rightly dividing God's Word is astonishing!

The Glorious Destiny Of Israel deals with Scripture as it relates to the children of Abraham. It examines the promises and prophecies God made exclusively to Israel. It sees the Bible solely from a Jewish perspective. These Chosen of God will remain after the Rapture. The purpose of this book is to present "the other side of the coin." God is faithful and always keeps His promises. The book examines these promises made to Israel and shows how God will ultimately fulfill them.

About The Author

Dr. Greene worked for more than thirty-five years as an independent insurance agent. He managed a multi-state agency selling all types of insurance. Now, he devotes his time to studying and teaching  the Bible. He holds that the Bible is the authoritative, inspired, and complete Word of God.

He studied at Evangelical Theological Seminary where he received his Bachelor of Theology, Master of Biblical Studies, and Ph.D. in Biblical Studies. He received a second Ph.D. in Christian Counseling through the National Association of Christian Counselors. Currently, he is serving as Dean of Graduate Studies at Evangelical Theological Seminary.

www.ingramcontent.com/pod-product-compliance
Lightning Source LLC
Chambersburg PA
CBHW070750120626
46557CB00002B/523